Managing acquisitions
in library and information services

Revised edition

Liz Chapman

facet publishing

D1173721

© Liz Chapman, 1989, 2001, 2004

Published by Facet Publishing,
7 Ridgmount Street, London WC1E 7AE
www.facetpublishing.co.uk

Facet Publishing is wholly owned by CILIP: the Chartered Institute of Library and Information Professionals.

British Library Cataloguing in Publication Data
A catalogue record for this book is available from the British Library.

ISBN 978-1-85604-496-7

First published 1989 as *Buying books for libraries*
Second edition 2001
This revised edition 2004
Reprinted 2008

Typeset from author's disks in 11/15pt Elegant Garamond and Humanist 521 by Facet Publishing.
Printed and made in Great Britain by MPG Books Ltd, Bodmin, Cornwall.

Contents

List of figures

The following organizations kindly gave permission to reproduce illustrations:

Blackwell's	Figures 2.3, 2.4
Dawson	Figures 3.1, 5.1, 7.1, 8.4, 9.1, 9.4
Ex-Libris	Figure 8.5
IS Oxford	Figures 6.2, 6.3, 7.2, 9.5
SIRSI	Figures 8.1, 9.2
TALIS	Figures 2.2, 5.2, 6.1, 8.2, 9.3

Acknowledgements

Work on this revised edition has been greatly helped by friends and colleagues who have given generously of their time to support my efforts. Acknowledgements from previous versions still stand.

At the Taylor Institution Library in Oxford I would like to thank Liz Baird, David Thomas, Jill Hughes and John Wainwright, who gave specialist help and knowledge freely. From other libraries in Oxford John Wagstaff and Liz Martin helped in updating specialist sections, while Antony Brewerton of Oxford Brookes University did the same. Others who provided specialist input and support include Anthony Watkinson, Vincent Matthews, Linda Bennett, Enrico Martellini, Norman Desmarais and Mo Siewcharran. Help with providing new illustrations came from Emma Duffield, Maggie McNair, George Hammond, Alan Oliver, David Thomas, Ken Chad and Carol Mansley. Any errors in the text, however, can only be laid at my door.

Completing the revision came at a difficult time for me and I would like to acknowledge the crucial support of my Deputy at the Taylor, Amanda Peters, who made it possible for me to grapple with all the last-minute checking, Sue Usher, who enquired tactfully from time to time how it was going, and, of course, my husband, Frank Webster, who set the pace by working on several books at once. I missed my mother's determined encouragement, but hope she would have approved the results.

Much of the preliminary research for the revision was carried out in the Library at University College London. The end of work on this revision marks the end of a very happy period as a Professorial Fellow of Somerville College, Oxford. Without the intellectual stimulation, office space and friendship this provided I doubt whether I would have completed the work necessary, and I offer my grateful thanks for their true fellowship.

I
Introduction

This revised edition provides an updated introduction to the practice of acquisitions in library and information services. It is intended for those who do not have much experience of acquisitions work, including students, and for those who want to improve or revise their acquisitions practice. Although it has been written largely from the perspective of someone who has worked in academic libraries, it should be applicable to different types of service and should be of more than passing interest to library suppliers, system suppliers and publishers. Although the practical principles of the first edition still hold in the second, this book brings acquisitions practice up to date, as so much of that practice is carried on over the internet.

This is not a book which concerns itself with materials selection or collection development as such, but concentrates on the process of acquiring materials. The word 'management' in the title refers to the management of the process of acquisitions, and not the management of the acquisitions staff. The underlying theme is that of communication between the various parties involved in the process. Acquisitions holds the key to communication with work colleagues, including finance officers, system suppliers, publishers, and suppliers and, most importantly, with the users of the materials they are involved in acquiring. Improving the channels of communication undoubtedly improves service at all stages.

What is acquisitions?

Acquisitions forms a vital link in the cycle of publishing, selection, request and providing materials for use. The imperatives for acquisitions staff are to find and acquire material as quickly and as economically as possible, while offering an efficient and responsive service. The effective acquisitions section is founded on nurturing successful relationships with those outside and inside the workplace. To other information staff acquisitions looks like the most desk-bound of occupations, since links are not so often made with the users of the material being bought.

In reality acquisitions staff have to learn to deal with a variety of people apart from their immediate colleagues. Good ethical relationships with suppliers and publishers are fundamental, but so too are links with finance officers, accountants and auditors. Being in control of a budget brings responsibility and a measure of power. A head for figures and a memory for titles, an ability to negotiate a licence or a good discount, and enhanced skills in using automation to speed the process and report on results, are just some of the attributes needed for acquisitions. The detective skills of reference staff, the descriptive skills of cataloguers, and the common-sense skills of the realist, are all equally required. Like all information staff, acquisitions people need to keep up with what is happening inside their workplace, but also outside in the world of publishing – and a good deal is happening.

Early automation of library systems tended to bolt acquisitions onto cataloguing, and acquisitions became a lesser part of technical or bibliographical services sections. Nowadays, however, acquisitions are first-line cataloguers, as orders are loaded onto the online system ahead of their actual arrival. And it is acquisitions staff who check online services for bibliographic details ahead of ordering and receipt. Integrated library systems with multi-functioning single workstations which communicate electronically all the way along the chain are rapidly becoming the norm. If there is a sticking point in total integration it is the interface with institutional finance systems. Much more acquisitions information is now held with, and accessible from, our suppliers. Acquisitions staff need to balance the loss of tedious record-keeping work with the potential loss of control over data.

Not only are more acquisitions processes being automated but the very materials being ordered are changing. No longer is acquisitions simply concerned with physical format such as hardback or paperback books, but choices are now much more complex between print and electronic. There are even staff now who deal solely with electronic acquisitions. Should material be purchased outright or simply on an online subscription? If only access is paid for, what kind of licence or contract applies and for how long? Deciding how to buy, whether from the usual supplier or vendor, or from one of the new internet or web bookstores, or from some hybrid version of both, extends and challenges the expertise of acquisitions staff. Increasingly, too, serials and periodicals are becoming part of acquisitions but this book does not deal with serials except in passing. The concept of a hybrid collection with a mixture of formats leads to interesting complexities and considerations in acquisitions work.

How this book is arranged

This is essentially a practical book and most chapters are provided with further reading to help you discover more about the topics covered. References to works mentioned in the text are given in a list at the end of the book. A glossary of some of the most common acronyms and terms used in acquisitions is also provided. Illustrations and examples are just that and should not necessarily be taken as endorsement. I have expressly avoided giving a list of possible systems suppliers or materials suppliers, as it would be impossible to be exhaustive and the market for both is frequently changing. I hope that this book gives you enough information to be able to find out who they are, what they offer and to make up your own mind about what is best for your service.

This book intends to pick a logical pathway along the route of acquisitions, passing by pre-order checking, publishing, information on non-standard materials, choosing, using and evaluating suppliers, ordering in its many guises, claiming, receiving and paying. Along the way it provides checklists and illustrations of procedures. The final chapter advises on how to keep up with this fast-moving field. Reading this book should help you to understand the role of acquisitions in its context, and to improve service in terms of speed, cost, efficiency and financial competence. I hope that it also shows how interesting and rewarding acquisitions work can be. There is always more to learn in an area which necessarily embraces change.

2
Pre-order checking

The real beginning of the acquisitions process is dealing with requests to purchase, searching local records to see if the item is already in stock or on order, and verifying the details needed to create an order.

Requests to purchase

Requests come in many guises, from e-mail to word of mouth, from scribbled notes to marked-up publishers' catalogues, from a newspaper cutting to a student's reading list, from an author's self-recommendation to information from suppliers. Making such requests seems to be a seasonal occupation and requests come in peaks and troughs. Acquisitions staff need to make order out of the potential chaos, to prioritize and organize checking to speed up the process. Users have little idea of what needs to be done before material is ordered and will not always conform to the bureaucracy of the service, but this is an area where acquisitions staff do need to follow established procedures.

Request forms

The most common way to establish some control over requests is to reduce them all to a common format – that is, a request/recommendation/suggestion form. Designing such a form needs to take into account different factors and forces. On the broadest scale, what used to be simply a request form is now very commonly a multifunction form which will cover all the possibilities of: pre-order check, order input, receipt, claim, payment, cataloguing, processing and statistics collection. Forms do not have to be on paper, and providing an interactive web request form may be one way to persuade users it is worth completing. Although you may prefer requests to come on nice neat forms, you cannot (nor should you) always insist on it. One advantage of paper is that different colours can be used to track progress visually by month or year, department or fund account. Here are some of the factors to consider when designing a request form:

- ease of use
- logical checking route for acquisitions
- clear layout for order system input
- obvious headings for checking orders in process
- accessible space for notes on receipt
- suitability of use for claims and reports
- space for cataloguing use, e.g. barcode
- space for processing use, e.g. binding notes.

Provision of all the possible spaces staff might want to work on is hard to achieve without clutter, and all forms represent a compromise between competing needs. The form shown in Figure 2.1 is an amalgamation of forms developed through several different services. No form should be cast in concrete, but should be reviewed from time to time, even if it is a form provided by your suppliers. The design of online forms should try to stick to one screen as far as possible for economy of effort and accuracy of input.

Checking requests

The basic strategy for checking requests should not vary from item to item. Never believe what anyone outside your service tells you about what is in stock. You must always check. A slight variation in the title or publisher may make them overlook the fact that what they want is already there. Checking your own stock, or that of services in your group, is the first step towards avoiding unwanted duplication, or providing intentional duplication of very busy titles. The amount of detail noted on the form after this initial check will depend on your ordering policy, on the relationship with your supplier, on the availability of detailed information and to some extent on how urgently you need to process the order. You will certainly be aiming to verify before ordering: author, title, publisher, date, price, ISBN. The amount of detail needed for ordering is covered in Chapter 6. Figure 2.2 shows the kind of information needed for an automated order system.

It is sensible to capture and record as much information as possible when you make the initial checks, so that subsequent efforts do not have to be made just to

Order Request Form

Author:

Title:

Place: **Publisher:**   **Year:**

Series:

                  ISSN
                  ISBN HB
                  ISBN PB

Continuation with no s.o.?   yes /no

New edition? yes / no   **Price:**

Source of reference:

Order Details

On system ?   F / NF   **Supplier:**

If found, state where: **Fund:**

Local control number: **Order no:**

Date:

Order already made (by e-mail, other)?   yes / no

Donations

Donor's name: *please print, & include title (e.g. Prof.) & initials*

Member of Faculty? yes / no   **Acknowledged?** yes / no / no need

Notes:

Figure 2.1   Order request form

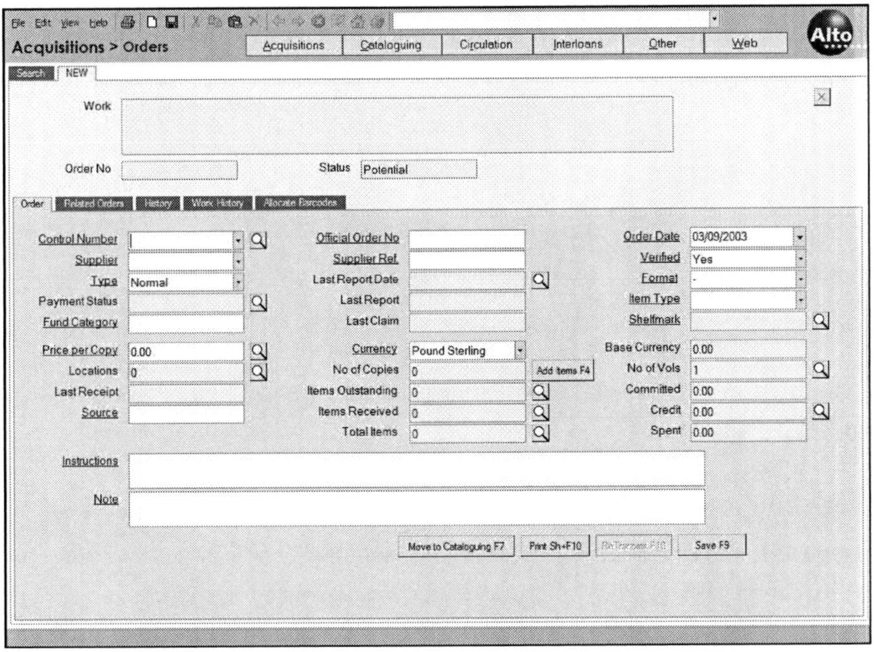

Figure 2.2 New order record ready for completion

verify a small but significant detail such as the ISBN. Adopting the convention of F meaning 'found' and NF meaning 'not found' avoids the ambiguity of a tick, cross or circle, which fails to distinguish between 'I have checked and found' and 'I have checked but not found'. The date of checking is also useful, as catalogues and bibliographies are constantly updated, and what was not there two weeks ago may now have appeared. The initials of the person making the check are also useful in case of later query.

Those who check requests, particularly in large services, need to understand that if some fundamental discrepancy between the request and the actual item is found – say, in the spelling of an author's name – then checking needs to return to square one. You may have the item by Phillips but not the one by Phipps.

Stock-checking

Request forms usually have an area for the user to fill in and a section for acquisitions staff to complete. It is best to leave features such as the price in the official part of the form unless you want that box filled up by the requester with comments like 'expensive' or 'unknown' where you ultimately want to record the price for ordering. Completion of the form should enable you to record whether the item is:

- a new edition
- a continuation/part of a series (see Chapter 4)
- a replacement
- an extra copy.

Noting the item's potential shelfmark or classification, or at least part of it, will speed later cataloguing.

Checking the catalogue

The public face of stock information is the catalogue. There are myriad rules for construction of catalogues but these do not always lead to ease of use. The use of AACR2 (*Anglo-American Cataloguing Rules*, 2nd edition) and MARC (machine-readable cataloguing) in the compilation of automated online catalogues has made catalogues somewhat easier to check, and an online catalogue can be accessed from anywhere with access to the relevant network.

Many information and library services store their records on joint databases. For example, the larger UK university library services combine their records on the CURL (Consortium of University and Research Libraries) database, known as COPAC when you check it online. Similarly the larger USA research libraries with some other international libraries have a combined RLG (Research Libraries Group) online database known as RLIN (Research Libraries Information Network). Some services combine their records via their automated system so they have a joint database of holdings searchable by members. Some take from and contribute their records on an international scale to commercial database utilities such as OCLC. Large co-operatives arrange access to other substantial catalogues such as LC (Library of Congress) or BNB (British National Bibliography) on behalf of their members. Some of these services charge for access on a subscription basis and/or charge for using a single record. More detail on some of the major services is given later in this chapter.

Close co-operation between acquisitions and cataloguing can economize on checking work and speed up the processing of materials when they arrive. It is usually the case that order records appear as part of the catalogue, to be edited and enhanced when the order arrives. Drawing up order records to conform with agreed cataloguing standards means extra training for acquisitions staff, but more importantly it means that users are alerted to new items before they arrive and can reserve them if they wish. In some services cataloguers or joint technical services staff, using a computer with all the necessary access points available at one workstation, create orders.

When checking the catalogue you should try to use a unique key such as the ISBN if possible, to save wading through many similar entries. Be aware of the following:

- variant spelling of authors' names, e.g. Webster, Webber, Wepster
- variants of the same author's name, e.g. 'Chapman, Liz' and 'Chapman, Elizabeth'
- items with more than three authors, or edited works – double-check the title
- individual titles that may be part of pre-existing collected works
- official bodies which may or may not be listed under a country's name, e.g. United Kingdom. Department of Health, United Nations. World Health Organization.

Checking beyond the catalogue

Stock-checking involves looking at the catalogue, the orders and those items in process which have arrived but may not yet be catalogued. Automation has greatly helped to avoid the 'limbo' where items have arrived but for some reason are not recorded, but be sure that you have covered all possibilities, including any unrecorded donations.

Suppliers as information sources

Library suppliers and online booksellers are increasingly becoming a good source of information on current and newly published material via their own specialist databases. Library suppliers also send out pre-publication e-mail alerts or information slips to acquisitions. These services can be expensive to run and, unless your profile is very carefully drawn, seldom hit the target exactly. Such supplier services are considered further in Chapter 5. The online bookstores have made a good job of drawing up customer profiles and alerting services, and, although not positively oriented towards the library market, are certainly having an effect on it. Figures 2.3 and 2.4 show a search for one author, and then pulling out further details of one title by that author using a library supplier's online system.

Reading lists

In academic libraries material often needs to be ordered from student reading lists. The most difficult part of this task is actually getting hold of the list of recommended reading. Dealing with these lists is basically the same as checking request forms, only worse. It is good to see that academic services are now putting their reading lists on their online information systems, and in some cases providing digitized versions of the material there too. Some lists are mini-books in themselves and do not repay hours of checking. Some are carefully compiled with the most important works highlighted. The advantage of checking and acting on lists is that you are thereby responding to student needs. On the negative side, lists can often be bibliographically unsound.

In the UK a service called HERON supports the online provision of copyright-cleared reading-list materials. HERON (Higher Education Resources ON-demand) is owned by Ingenta, a commercial intermediary company with access to large databases of digitized serials and other materials. HERON aims to act as a clearing house, providing copyright clearance, digitization and electronic delivery of journal articles and book extracts requested. It is intended to be accessed by library and information staff, academics, researchers and students.

Bibliographic data

If you cannot verify details for a request through your own catalogue, or through the services you can access by virtue of membership, supplier or subscription, you will need to use commercial bibliographical services. Here you are perhaps looking to check an author and title, but also more importantly to find details of price, date of publication, publisher and ISBN. The order in which you check bibliographies and databases will depend on the importance you place on trade information such as price and ISBN, as opposed to bibliographical information such as the correct form of an author's name. The provision of such bibliographical services is changing, and although library and information

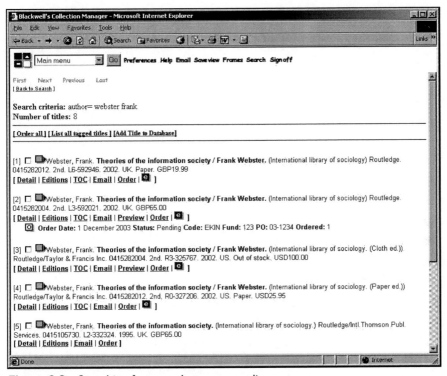

Figure 2.3   Searching for an author on a supplier system

Figure 2.4   Expanded information on one title

services are coming to depend increasingly on outside agencies providing this data, there is a considerable cost involved.

There are many different services that you can search online for order verification and it is not possible to describe them all here. Apart from a quick check on online booksellers' databases the most commonly used and accessible commercial services for English-language material from the UK and USA are briefly described. These are followed by UK and USA national bibliographies. Many such services are now available online. Traditional printed bibliographies still support browsing, serendipity, readability and, to some extent, portability, while online sources will be more up to date.

Using printed trade bibliographies requires a knowledge of their layout, as searching is much less sophisticated than in an online service. Look out for the following traps:

- Mac, Mc, M' all filed together but alphabetically at Mac
- double-barrelled surnames filed by the last or first part
- numerals filed as if spelled out – e.g. 10 may be found under 'ten'
- Dr, Mr, St filed as if spelled out – e.g. Dr will be found under 'doctor'
- filing word by word.

There is no substitute for using the instructions given with any bibliography.

Nielsen BookData

Nielsen BookData incorporates BookData, Whitaker Information Services and *first* Edition. They provide a range of bibliographic services, order routing and EDI services. Their databases consist of over five million records giving rich data including: literary awards, promotional information, cover images and market rights information for English language books published worldwide. They also provide web services for the book industry. Using *first* Edition's network and EDI, libraries and their suppliers can integrate electronic trading into their local systems and exchange electronic messages.

BookFind-Online

With over five million titles, this is a fully searchable web-based subscription service, updated daily and including information on titles recently out of print.

Users can select global coverage (*Premier*) to include USA, Australia, New Zealand and Southern Africa, or can opt for UK-only searches (*BookWise*). Records include titles, authors, prices, descriptions, tables of contents, cover images and publisher/distributor details, with MARC output for acquisitions purposes. This is an annual subscription service.

LibWeb

This service is tailored specifically for library use. A fully searchable web-based subscription service, *LibWeb* provides access to the most comprehensive, accurate listing of English language books published internationally. It offers information on over four million titles, updated daily, including information on titles recently out of print. Basic search results can be configured, sorted and displayed as required. Users can select global coverage to include USA, Australia, New Zealand and Southern Africa, or can opt for UK-only searches. This is an annual subscription service.

Both *BookFind-Online* and *LibWeb* offer full bibliographic records featuring extended descriptive content, including short and long descriptions, author biography, table of contents, reviews, wholesaler flagging, Dewey and BIC classification and over 140,000 cover images.

BookWise – CD-ROM

This CD-ROM resource covers 1.8 million English-language titles published or distributed in the UK and Ireland. *BookWise* offers extensive information on titles, including descriptions, tables of contents, subject codes and readership levels, plus information on the stockholding of all the major UK and Irish wholesalers. A special feature of this CD-ROM is the inclusion of the Booksellers Association's *Directory of UK & Irish Publishers*, which gives access to trade terms, contacts, distribution agreements, information on returns facilities and contracts. This product is available as a single disc service, on a monthly subscription.

Premier CD

Premier-CD provides comprehensive information for English-language books published internationally, with over 3.2 million English-language titles available in UK, Europe, US, Australia, New Zealand and Southern Africa. The high level of information offered includes descriptive summaries and tables of contents, publisher and distributor details, market rights information, literary awards, promotional information and selected jacket and book covers. Subject classifications include BIC, Library of Congress and Dewey classification. This product is available for subscription on a monthly basis.

Whitaker's Books in Print is no longer produced, either in hard copy or microfiche.

Bowker

Bowker, part of the Reed Business Information Group, is a source of online bibliographical data for the USA and beyond.

Booksinprint.com

This is the internet subscription version of *Books in Print*, with 2.4 million titles, including forthcoming titles and 800,000 out-of-print titles. This service is also available with reviews. It covers video and audio books, and gives contact information for 69,000 publishers. Searching is possible using title, subject, author, publisher and keywords. Records can be downloaded, and there are hyperlinks to authors and publishers, as well as subject classifications. An 'In the media' area allows checking of titles mentioned on USA television. Records can be downloaded by acquisitions in formats to suit different automated systems. Information is also available on stock availability for major US suppliers and wholesalers. A link can be made to your own online catalogue, thus cutting down the number of separate searches which acquisitions needs to make. A subscription to *Booksinprint.com* also allows free access to information on e-books and on-demand titles at *e-booksinprint.com*.

Global Books in Print (Globalbooksinprint.com)

This web service combines information from different national ISBN agencies. It provides information on more than eight million English-language titles from the USA, UK, Canada, Australia and New Zealand. Searching can be by LCSH and it is possible to compare prices and binding between all international editions of any one title, and locate over 165,000 publishers worldwide.

National bibliographies

If searching commercial bibliographies does not provide you with all the information you need, and if in particular you are looking for non-current material, you should turn to national bibliographies. These are compiled by people who know how to catalogue. Some European-language national bibliographies are described in Chapter 4.

The British Library

The *British National Bibliography* (*BNB*) exists to list and describe all new items published in the UK and the Republic of Ireland. It began in 1950, is the national bibliography for the UK and is based on copyright receipt. Under the UK Copyright Acts the British Library is entitled to receive one copy of every book and soon every electronic publication produced in the UK.

It is important to note what materials are not covered by *BNB*. It does not include periodicals (except the first issue), music, maps, publications without a UK imprint, and many regular UK government publications. Further information can be found in the prefatory material to the print version.

The major drawback of *BNB* as far as acquisitions is concerned is the delay before items get into the listing. Any kind of delay can of course impair the value of price information and it is always preferable to rely on trade bibliographies, suppliers' information or publishers' information for this.

A full *BNB* record will give the following: Dewey classmark, author, title, other authors (up to three), editor, edition, place of publication, publisher, date, number of pages, size, series, ISBN, price and *BNB* number. Its main value at the pre-order checking stage is for checking non-mainstream material. Smaller publishers which might not feature in trade bibliographies, and authors who publish their own works, may be found here, as well as a good deal of older material.

BNB includes a good deal of pre-publication information supplied by publishers. This is called Cataloguing in Publication (CIP) data and is compiled from pre-publication proofs or standard forms filled in by publishers before a book is published. The same information, or an alert to its existence, appears on the verso-title page of many newly published books. These records are clearly designated CIP and have outline cataloguing which is later upgraded when the item appears in the British Library. The prior announcement of titles can be problematic for acquisitions and is discussed further in Chapter 3.

BNB on CD-ROM

Containing some 1.7 million catalogue records, this service provides Dewey classmarks and LCSH. It cumulates and updates every month and includes some 50,000 CIP records. Internet access can be added, including links to the BL's own online catalogues and to many publishers. There are 25 search indexes, which can display results as a catalogue card and in full MARC. Records are from 1986 onwards. There is a backfile CD-ROM for 1950 to 1985.

Books in English

This microform service has been published every two months on microfiche and lists all titles from the *BNB*, plus those catalogued by the Library of Congress (LC). It started in 1971 and cumulates annually, but ceases publication in 2004, at which time it becomes a historical reference resource. In this service the control number is generally the ISBN. Numbers beginning B...... are *BNB* numbers, while numbers beginning LC...... are Library of Congress numbers, and those beginning DC are Dewey classmarks.

The general arrangement of the printed *BNB* is as follows. The first section is a Dewey-classified sequence. The second section, more useful to acquisitions, is an alphabetical listing by authors, titles, editors and series. These entries may be abbreviated, and in this case you have to take the Dewey number and check back to the full entry in the first section. The third section is a subject index. *BNB* has its own control numbers, which are sometimes used in book selection.

The Library of Congress

Library of Congress data for cataloguing that can also be used for ordering is supplied online by library suppliers, co-operatives and commercial services. It is an accepted international standard. Large library services may have access to the printed or microform versions for checking called *The National Union Catalog* or NUC for short.

This is the USA counterpart to *BNB*. It is an alphabetical catalogue by author or editor and title, originally printed from reproduced catalogue cards from the Library of Congress in Washington, DC, and involving 1,000 other large libraries in the USA. It started in 1876. It is available as a monthly cumulating microfiche service with annual cumulations. The best way to approach a search in this service is to use the indexes (name, title, subject and series), which will direct you to the fuller entry, although it may be that the register entry is enough for acquisitions purposes. Bear in mind that whether you are using NUC online, microfiche or print versions, these are basically cataloguing, not acquisitions services, so you will not be able to confirm order details such as prices. However, you can produce a ready-made catalogue record, which will only need minimal editing when your order arrives. LC data includes all major USA publications, trade and government publications, and entries for items which LC collects actively all over the world. It is therefore worth checking for non-English-language material.

Keeping up with sources old and new

It should be clear from the above that many different services are of use for pre-order checking. It is also true that the nature and ownership of these sources change from time to time. For acquisitions it is sensible to collect your most frequently used services as icons on your computer desktop, or at least to bookmark them for ease of access. It is increasingly difficult to keep up with all the new internet services without the help of like-minded colleagues. *AcqWeb* and *BUBL*, for example, can help locate services and make links to the most useful ones, but they are somewhat daunting at first glance. Printed directories are now firmly bypassed by online information, either from commercial publishers or from your suppliers. You will need to note individual services that are useful to acquisitions and check every so often for new ones.

3
Publishers and publishing

Much is changing in the world of publishing, and it would be wrong to look at how to use information from publishers to improve acquisitions work without considering the shifting scenery. Library and information staff seldom meet with publishers and the work of each group is almost invisible to the other, except in the shape of publishers' products, and these are evolving rapidly.

Publishers for the most part work in the commercial world, and work to make profits. The profit on printed books is, however, not as high as that on products in other retail trades. The profit on journals is a much more serious bone of contention between publishers and librarians. Publishers have recently been prone to an unprecedentedly high level of mergers, take-overs and consequent redundancies. The larger ones are multinational companies controlling a substantial part of the industry, even though this may not be apparent on bookshelves, as they use many different individual imprints. Booksellers themselves can have an effect on what is published, as major retail chains are now very large.

Trade publishers which produce high-selling popular books look to print-runs of 10,000 to 100,000. Scholarly publishers working on academic texts look at print-runs nearer the 1000 mark. Reference publishing may be nearer 10,000 depending on the topic. Smaller 'alternative' publishers may have very small print-runs, and their output may be harder to trace and purchase. It is for this reason that acquisitions staff need to be rapidly aware of what is available before it goes out of print. The library market for books is only around 10% of all publishing output.

While the number of books being published remains high, changes are happening in what is being published, which challenge publishers and acquisitions alike. As libraries try to decide which way to jump in the access v ownership debate – should we provide access to a text rather than buy it outright? – the product itself is changing. Books now appear with or as discs, DVDs or CD-ROMs, some journals appear only electronically, and electronic books or e-books are evolving and gaining acceptability.

Electronic materials

Publishers' electronic products can go straight to the user, bypassing any intermediary information or library service. Some materials are produced simultaneously in print and electronically; some are exact reproductions of the same text, but care has to be taken when electronic products are being purchased to check what has been bundled up together. Acquisitions staff need to be sure that they know whether they are intentionally buying something already in stock in another format, what licensing may be required and what can be archived. Journals are increasingly available electronically and books are moving, albeit more slowly, in that direction. There is more on e-books in Chapter 7.

Checking the attributes of electronic materials before purchase should include the following considerations, although if you need the material you may have to compromise on your highest expectations:

1 **Full-text/original text/comprehensiveness.** Does this product offer the original printed text with all illustrations?
2 **Accuracy/authority.** Does this product have the same high standards as previous printed materials?
3 **Ease of use.** Will this material require training/marketing for users/staff?
4 **Availability.** Is this product available at all times with good connections if internet access is required?
5 **Updating.** Is this product likely to be updated and if so how?
6 **Archiving.** Can this material be archived?
7 **Pricing.** Is there a differential pricing regime for different numbers of users?
8 **Licensing.** What are the licensing requirements and liabilities?

Information on publishers

There are several standard directories of publishers which are helpful if you need to contact a publisher direct, although many use intermediary companies to handle distribution, and increasing numbers have websites. Websites of individual publishers mean that the directories listed here are decreasingly necessary. Publisher websites are evolving beyond simple advertising and now encompass internal information on an intranet, password protected business-to-business information, and marketing and sales information for customers.

Directory of UK and Irish Book Publishers

Details of 3000 publishers, listed alphabetically, with ordering information, ISBN prefixes, contact information and www addresses. This is available via the Booksellers Association website and via Nielsen BookData's BookWise service.

International Literary Market Place

Book publishing information for 180 countries world-wide outside the USA and Canada. Also includes booksellers and major libraries.

Literary Market Place

Information on the USA publishing scene, featuring publishers, agents, distributors and events, contact information and www addresses. Available in print, CD-ROM and internet versions.

Publishers' Directory

Information on more than 20,000 USA and Canadian publishers, large and small, including electronic publishers, distributors, wholesalers and suppliers

Publishers, Distributors and Wholesalers of the US

Information on 10,000 USA publishers from large to small, including those recently gone out of business. Can be searched by imprint name.

Whitaker's 'Red Book'

This directory lists up to 4000 publishers, distributors and wholesalers in the UK and Ireland. It also lists library suppliers and provides dates of international book fairs as well as giving information on the ISBN Agency.

Information from publishers

ISBNs

International Standard Book Numbers (ISBNs) are one of the most important pieces of information you can get from publishers. They act as unique identifiers for single published items and are crucial in ordering, so must be discovered if at all possible at the pre-order checking stage. ISBNs were first used in the UK in 1967 and will therefore not be found on books published before that date. They are to be revised in future as described below. There are separate ISBNs for paperback and hardback versions of the same title, and for different editions. There are separate ISBNs for different publishers of the same work – for example, when the same book is published simultaneously in the UK and the USA. It is possible, therefore, for the same text to have four different ISBNs, depending on the publisher and the binding. The picture is even more complex for series (see Chapter 4).

The importance of an ISBN

ISBNs are crucial in the ordering of books because publishers and their distributors use them for the picking of stock. If you quote the wrong ISBN, you could well get the wrong book. Although it is not a total disaster to get a cookery book for an economics research library, or a manual for dentists for a European literature collection, it may well be a waste of time. ISBNs are also crucial because they are often used as control numbers in automated systems. Worryingly, it is possible for publishers to reallocate ISBNs from one text to another, but this does not happen very often. You can complete or decode an unknown ISBN by using the *Publishers' International ISBN Directory*, which covers some 584,000 publishers in more than 210 countries.

The structure of an ISBN

Every ISBN consists of ten digits, and may be quoted in orders as a simple string of numbers, or may be divided into four parts by dashes or spaces. The four parts of the number are made up as shown in the following examples:

1   **Group identifier** (national or language), e.g.:

    0 or 1   UK, USA, Australia, Canada, New Zealand

    2   France; French-speaking Belgium, Canada, Switzerland

3	Austria, Germany, German-speaking Switzerland
4	Japan
5	Russia
6	China
91	Sweden
92	international organizations
958	Colombia
978	Nigeria.

2   **Publisher prefix**, e.g.:

| 19 | Oxford University Press |
| 85381 | Virago. |

NB the length of the publisher identifier tends to be in inverse proportion to the output of the publisher. It is simply a case of first come, first served, and larger publishers joined first.

3   **Title identifier.**
4   **Check digit**
    This is always the last digit, used by automated systems to validate the whole ISBN against transcription errors. The check digit X denotes 10.

The European Article Numbering (EAN) standard converts the ISBN into a barcode, which is printed on the back of many books and used in retail stocktaking. The International Organization for Standardization (ISO) is currently working on changes that need to be made to the ISBN for the digital age. New 13-digit ISBNs are planned for 2007, which will incorporate the EAN standard. Changes are needed because available numbers are running out and there is pressure to provide metadata for electronic editions. At the same time, changes will be made to the administration of the ISBN to ensure the long-term viability of the system and its application in the more than 160 agencies which allocate ISBNs.

Publishers' catalogues

Not so long ago, acquisitions sections needed to store substantial numbers of publishers' catalogues. These are produced mainly for booksellers, but are useful for pre-order checking if you need up-to-date information on new and projected publications. Time used to be spent getting hold of these catalogues too. Now things are changing as publishers have websites where much information can be found. *AcqWeb* provides a very useful directory of publishers' websites as well as a publisher e-mail address directory. If you need to use a particular website often, you should bookmark it on your own computer. Even small publishers without a substantial internet presence can be found on the web via the online bookstores.

Publisher websites are not yet ubiquitous, nor indeed uniformly useful, and it will probably be some time before the glossy publisher's catalogue completely disappears. You will still receive these and will need to request them from time to time. Websites and printed catalogues alike carry the same health warning: the information is only as good as that provided to the editor or compiler. The tag 'new' against a title is sometimes misleading and can mean any of the following:

- a reprint of a previously published item
- a paperback reprint
- a title new to this publisher that previously existed with another
- a title previously announced but still not published
- a new edition
- a new title.

Publishers' blurbs

Fliers or blurbs describing single items or series will continue to arrive by post from publishers and are often used as the basis for requests to purchase. The ideal catalogue entry or blurb will give you enough information from which to order the item and should have:

- a description of the contents
- the intended audience
- a description of the author
- bibliographic data, including ISBN
- availability details.

Publishers' representatives

Library and information staff are seldom visited by publishers' representatives, who spend their days in the more lucrative aisles of the retail bookseller. However, if you are offered a visit, and you can make a convenient appointment, it is recommended that you do. The rep's concerns may well be sales and price, whereas yours may be availability, but on the whole we have a lot to learn from each other. Reps visit other services too, and make a good unofficial grapevine. From time to time you may have useful information to give publishers on what might be missing from their lists.

Book fairs and exhibitions

The most famous international book fair is the Frankfurt Book Fair, which is held in the Autumn. It is basically a forum for publishers to show their wares and to make deals on publishing rights. There is a similarly important annual fair in Bologna for children's books. The most important book fair in the UK is the London Book Fair, which happens in the Spring. None of these fairs is well attended by library and information staff. Modest entrance fees include catalogues listing exhibitors, which can become useful additions to your address book later on. Most exhibitors are publishers but there are some dealers, agents and other allied businesses. They make good occasions on which to pick up really recent information, but the size of the exhibit halls makes it impossible to do justice to all of it.

Another very large but more diverse exhibition is that attached to the American Library Association conferences, which take place in Summer and Winter. Some publishers have substantial display stands and author signings. In the UK CILIP has a biennial conference with an exhibition which has some publisher stands. There are other more specialist fairs and exhibitions attached to conferences, which you can find out about through the professional press.

If you can get information about who will have stands before you attend an exhibition, this is helpful as you can then plan your visit properly. If not, take time when you get the catalogue to mark up the stands you want to see. Take with you information (or lack of it) on materials you need to check, and also take sticky labels with your name and address along with some business cards. The sticky labels can be used to avoid filling in all those forms with impossibly small boxes for your name and address, and the business cards can be dropped into prize draws in the vain hope that you win an e-book or something worse.

Checking for unpublished material

The words 'unpublished material' may seem like a contradiction in terms, but one of the functions of pre-order checking is to discover the availability or non-availability of material you need to order. Non-availability could mean either that something is not yet published, or that it has gone out of print, or that the publication has been abandoned. The first two are not entirely hopeless cases. Some requests in these categories might be very vague, along the lines of 'Has volume 16 of that series appeared yet?' or 'Is there a new edition of x?' or 'Has my favourite author published another murder mystery yet?'

Not yet published

The most common source of information on items which have not yet been published is information from the publisher in the form of blurbs, catalogues, or e-mail alerts, as already mentioned. This is generally promotional or advertising and needs to be viewed in that light. It would be invidious to mention names here, but you will soon get to realize which publishers give the longest lead time for their books. Suffice it to say that this kind of information circulates wherever acquisitions staff get together, and publishers who 'cry book' too soon get a bad reputation. Of course this does not solve the problem of the requester who has seen something advertised in a catalogue when the projected publication date has gone by and you are still not buying it for them.

Many publishers provide pre-publication information on books to their national libraries for cataloguing purposes. National libraries in turn provide Cataloguing in Publication (CIP) data, which is sometimes printed on the verso title page of the book on publication. Increasingly, however, there is simply a notice saying CIP information is available for this book. More important for pre-order checking purposes is the fact that this information is available in national bibliographies before the book is published, in countries which do not have long backlogs in publishing their national bibliographies. For the UK and the USA the bibliographies which hold this type of information are described in Chapter 2. Some European-language national bibliographies are described in Chapter 4.

Apart from supplying pre-publication information to cataloguing agencies, publishers also provide this information to the trade. You will therefore be able to find UK pre-publication information in *Books in print*, which gives a two-month lead time. The weekly lists in *The Bookseller* also have early warning information. Not to be overlooked are the special substantial January and November issues of *The Bookseller*, which include announcements for the following six months. For the USA, *Publishers Weekly* performs a similar function. You will need to decide whether to commit or encumber funds for material which is not yet published, when you could be spending the money on published items. On the other hand, publishers sometimes offer substantial pre-publication discounts which you can find via your system supplier, as Figure 3.1 shows.

Authors

Acquisitions staff need detective and professional skills, and need to use the resources they find around them on the internet and on reference shelves. There are probably services available to users which will help you to discover the whereabouts of elusive authors, or rather the authors of elusive titles. The

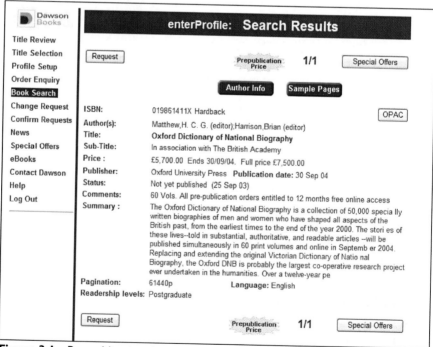

Figure 3.1   Pre-publication discounts checked via supplier

International Who's Who of Authors and Writers and *The Writers' Directory* are pre-eminent in their field, but if you do not have access to these, *Who's Who* will help you to trace the more popular English-language authors.

If you are trying to trace the whereabouts of academic authors you can use the *Commonwealth Universities Yearbook*, which lists academic staff, and senior library and information staff, in commonwealth universities. It has excellent indexes by subject and by name. For the USA you should try the *Directory of American Scholars* and the *National Faculty Directory*. *The World of Learning* includes institutes of higher education throughout the world, but although it lists senior staff, there is no name index in the print version.

These are only a few rather general possibilities but in your own subject field there will be some kind of 'Who's who' that you will find useful as there are 'Who's who' volumes for many countries of the world. If these suggestions are not helpful, you should check whether your elusive author has published before. If he or she has, you may get some information from the previous publisher. You may be able to contact the author via that publisher. Do not feel worried about contacting authors direct – they are generally flattered by the attention, although they may start laughing about books they have not even finished writing when you say you want to buy a copy.

Out-of-print material

Out-of-print material is another area where a little knowledge of cataloguing goes a long way, and also where the internet is helping in pre-order checking, and in ordering (see Chapter 7). Before ordering an out-of-print title it is still important to follow the usual pre-order checking route to verify bibliographical details. This can seem frustrating on a title-by-title basis, but the rewards are ordering the correct material for the person who wants it. For the UK and USA, the sources described in Chapter 2 for in-print materials also cover those recently out of print. For the USA Bowker's *Books Out of Print* covers more than a million titles which have gone out of print or out of stock indefinitely since 1979. It can be searched by author, ISBN, keyword, publisher, year of publication and other keys. Another source you should think about using is the catalogues of other collections, many of which you can check online as described in Chapter 2, and suppliers' databases as described in Chapter 5.

Some OP items may be available as microform or as reprints – these are considered in Chapter 7. Electronic products have certainly overtaken microform in user popularity – easy searching of the full text is only one reason for this – but you must take care not to order versions of a text which you have already as part of another product.

4

Beyond the basic book

A change of form

Methods for identifying, verifying and ordering traditional books and other print materials are well established. However, there are plenty of other formats that acquisitions will have to deal with, some old and some new. Non-book materials, as they are sometimes called, include the following: microform, audio-cassettes, video, film, music CDs, CD-ROMs, DVDs, software, databases and evolving e-books. Not only are these types of material more difficult to trace by the usual checking routes, but they also require special attention when they arrive, by way of equipment and training in use.

A request for such a purchase typically lacks the product details needed for ordering, such as title, cost, publisher and technical set-up details. Added to this, new products in different formats often overlap existing print versions and duplication needs to be avoided, or confirmed. If you are ordering a database, you will need to be sure it can be networked, whether on your own local area network, or whether as part of a national or consortium licensing agreement. If print and electronic versions are produced at the same time, which should be purchased? If you do not want to order for your local collection, how can you access the material elsewhere? Interlibrary loan is not always a straightforward answer in this field, but is it possible to share a subscription? Consortium purchasing is considered in Chapter 5.

Basic acquisition functions can change considerably as formats change. Scanning and digitization may take the place of acquisition, while networking takes the place of physical delivery. Online web resources need metadata instead of more traditional cataloguing, and preservation can be threatened, not by crumbling paper but by digital equipment obsolescence.

Some texts are already available on the internet as e-books. Originally these were generally older, out-of-print classic texts and reference works which are held in collections such as the *Gutenberg Project* in the USA or *Bibliomania* in the UK. E-book services are now developing which offer books both old and new in electronic formats for a subscription fee. Library suppliers may act as agents for you in buying in these services. However, some 'books' are now being published only on the internet, which poses even more acquisitions problems. There is more on electronic texts in Chapter 7.

Some hard-to-trace materials are known collectively as 'grey literature'. This covers a multitude of different types and formats, and the word 'grey' also describes the effect on your hair if you spend too long trying to check their whereabouts. Also known as 'fugitive literature', such materials can include reports, working papers, conference papers and proceedings, official publications, trade literature, pressure-group publications, privately published material, theses, translations and more. The internet is helpful in checking on many of these, and there is a useful website from the USA for alternative press material called *Counterpoise*. For all these sorts of material, including the more difficult print material mentioned later in this chapter, it is useful to bookmark internet sites and collect specialist publishers' catalogues to speed verification and ordering. The book is not yet dead, but new digital electronic materials are certainly alive and kicking. This chapter cannot cover all the different types of more diverse material in any depth, but gives a brief introduction to publications in series, some European language resources, UK government publications, music and other audiovisual materials.

Other collections

If you are not a specialist in an area where you have requests to order, then it makes sense to contact those who are. Most large collections have internet sites. You should collect information, bookmark those sources which are useful, and be prepared to return favours if asked. This is not to say that you should frequently take advantage of the goodwill of other services, but if you have tried the normal checking routes and drawn a blank, then a specialist collection may well help you out. Your reference and reader services colleagues should have access to the standard reference works about reference works. Electronic discussion lists are also helpful for gathering and sharing information.

There are several published directories for library and information services which may be useful here. For the USA there is the *Directory of Special Libraries and Information Centers*, while for Europe you can try the *Directory of University Libraries in Europe*. The *World Guide to Libraries* and the *World Guide to Special Libraries* are international in scope. For the UK you can use the *Aslib Directory of Information Sources in the United Kingdom* (Reynard, 2002), which has collection descriptions, but if you are only looking for service names and addresses, use Facet Publishing's annual *Libraries and Information Services in the United Kingdom and the Republic of Ireland*. The UK National Acquisitions Group's *Directory of Acquisitions Librarians in the United Kingdom and Republic of Ireland* (2003) gives names of staff who actually work in acquisitions in the UK and Ireland.

Series and continuations

Series and continuations are notoriously difficult to check and verify, falling as they do somewhere between monographs and serials. Standing orders for such materials are dealt with in Chapter 7. A continuation, in the context of pre-order checking, is something which supplements your existing holdings. If you already have volume 3 of a set of memoirs, a continuation would be either volumes 1 and 2, or 4 onwards. It is likely that all volumes in this set will be on one particular topic. Individual volumes may have individual titles. It is also possible that each volume will have its own ISBN, and there may be one ISBN to cover the whole set. On top of this there may also be an ISSN for the collection. ISSNs are generally allocated to serials or periodicals, which, although not the real subject of this book, can be defined as publications issued in indefinitely ongoing parts.

Series are also linked groups of material, but probably of a more disparate nature. They will carry a series title, but individual titles are likely to be by different authors, and there may be no foreseeable end to the series. There may be an overall series editor and although that name may stay for a long time, the series may well outlive the first editor and a new editor arrive on the scene. Series can appear regularly – for example, annually.

Unfortunately it is quite possible for items in a series to appear irregularly, and without the individual items in the series being numbered in any way. It is also possible for a series to be supplementary to what is otherwise a normal serial, e.g. supplements to a daily newspaper. Items in a series may be non-monographic but nevertheless numbered, e.g. the *Letters of Charles Dickens* from Oxford University Press. They may appear in small instalments which are not monographic, but are divided for publishing convenience into what are termed fascicles. Of course they may not be monographic at all because they are not books. Music is often produced in series as well as in numbered volumes.

The irregularity of appearance, and the fact that even if they do appear regularly they may not be in the correct sequence, can make continuations and series difficult to stock-check and trace. You should approach such checking carefully and verify as many of the following as you can:

- series title
- individual volume title
- editor(s)
- author(s)
- subject, e.g. *Modern Art in Britain*
- ISBN
- ISSN
- order records
- standing order records.

You may think that you are checking a straightforward request, which turns out to be part of a series. Watch out for the signs which betray this, including the following in the title:

- Advances in . . .
- Annual . . .
- Almanac . . .
- Developments in . . .
- Library of . . .
- . . . papers on . . .
- Progress in . . .
- . . . series
- Studies in . . .
- World . . .
- Yearbook of . . .

. . . or any of these preceded by 'International' or the name of a publisher.

You may find that you have to use extra sources to check series, and there are websites, publishers' catalogues and some national bibliographies which can help. Prices can also be difficult to trace, not least because many series are not mainstream trade publications but come from learned societies. A direct approach to the producer may be needed. Some subscription agents provide catalogues of serials, which include some series, free to their customers, and these are very helpful. These are usually searchable via the supplier's database. The Swets serials listing and database is one such example. There are also commercially produced directories of serials, and large research libraries will have correspondingly extensive serials holdings; it is worth checking these online. While the latter may provide bibliographical information more readily, they will not have information on prices.

It is not the purpose of this book to provide a guide on how to buy serials, but as continuations and series waver somewhere between books and journals, it is as well to know some of the tricks of the serials trade. Ordering of series and continuations is dealt with in Chapter 7.

Conferences

Conference proceedings consist of several individual contributions (or papers) prepared for a meeting, and if they are published there will generally be an editor. They are in themselves often part of a series, although there are also single conferences. Conference reports may appear as a special issue of a journal, so take care not to order something you already have on subscription. The latter information is not always discernible, however. Conferences may be announced with one title and then when they are published – maybe up to a year or more later – the title has changed. Tell-tale phrases which betray a conference include:

- Annals of . . .
- Conference on . . .
- Proceedings of . . .
- Seminar . . .
- Society of . . .
- Symposium on . . .
- Transactions of . . .

. . . or any of the above preceded by the words 'International' or 'Annual'.

You may be asked to order a pre-print or meeting paper, which is the text of a paper prepared before, and perhaps handed out during the conference, as opposed to the edited published version. Actually, editing conference proceedings is a long and arduous business, as the first task is to get all the authors to contribute properly written versions of their papers. Some authors will not meet deadlines and others will want to publish elsewhere. Short print-runs are also common, but equally it is becoming more common to see proceedings appear on the internet. If you only have a reference to one paper, but want to order the whole conference, you should use the online citation indexes to find the full reference. A single paper may be better obtained via interlibrary loan. Conferences can be traced via the internet sites of the organizers as well as via standard national bibliographies and the catalogues of other collections. The British Library has an extensive collection of conference proceedings and these can be traced and purchased via their *Inside* system, using the *zetoc* service. These services cover over 21,000 journals. Finally, if you are still having difficulty locating the conference papers you want, there are two other possibilities. First, try asking someone from your institution, or the requester, for more information. Secondly, not all conferences that are announced actually take place, nor do speakers turn up or even write their papers, so if in doubt contact the organizers direct.

Reports and working papers

Reports and working papers are a kind of series usually written for a particular audience, and they describe recent research or action taken or intended. One specific form of report is a law report, but these are less likely to be single items for purchase. Quasi-legal reports, however, which set out a programme of work to be carried out after signing a contract, may indeed need to be ordered. Government and other official and unofficial bodies often publish reports, and some methods of checking for these are described elsewhere in this chapter. A common form of report in the academic world is a discussion, seminar or working paper, which gives the results of recent research but is perhaps not yet suitable for a fully fledged publication. This kind of working paper is also common in commercial companies, banks and international organizations. Commercial companies, charities and other organizations publish annual reports, which can be treated as standing orders, and can often be obtained at little or no cost. At the other end of the scale, market research reports are often priced prohibitively and some government reports will be unobtainable as they are classified.

The unifying feature of reports is usually the date and/or some sort of identifying code number. This number is usually crucial if you want to order the right publication. It used to be the case that many reports were poorly produced and provided preservation problems, but increasingly reports and working papers are appearing on the internet. This method of internet publication is a boon, as previously many organizations' reports had very short print-runs. Known in this context as e-prints, and their holding areas known as institutional archives, these electronic papers have an interesting effect on conventional publishing, since they no longer actually appear in print, nor indeed need you own them. If you are not a specialist collector of reports and need advice on ordering, check with a service that is. If your institution produces reports, you have a responsibility to make sure that you have access to a complete set. A general service which may help you trace some reports is *SIGLE* (*System for Information on Grey Literature in Europe*).

European language materials

If you are buying from other countries it is useful to collect publishers' website addresses and catalogues and those from specialist dealers. For non-specialists the following sections may be helpful for initial checking of requests for material in French, German, Spanish, Italian and Portuguese. Use *AcqWeb* to help you find specialist suppliers. Where a national library catalogue appears on the internet, the use of commercial, CD-ROM or printed bibliographies is dwindling. *Gabriel* provides an internet gateway to European national libraries. The University of Queensland *Cybrary* website provides comprehensive access to national library catalogues. First Search's *WorldCat* is a useful international source of bibliographical information and the RLG *Union Catalog* provides access to several substantial non-English language supplier databases. Many antiquarian and secondhand suppliers have a presence on the internet.

French

Materials in French are published in France, Belgium and Switzerland as well as Canada and francophone Africa. It is also a published second language in Vietnam, Cambodia and the Lebanon. French library suppliers provide good sources of information on the internet.

National library catalogue

Bibliothèque Nationale de France (BNF) (www.bnf.fr)

The French national library catalogue is available online with the name *BN-OPALE PLUS* and covers books, audiovisual materials, maps, music, manuscripts, films, prints, currency collections and photographs. Some 70,000 images are digitally available on its *Gallica* website (http://gallica.bnf.fr). It was the first national library to put whole books online – they are currently free of charge for private use. A pay-per-view system for copyrighted books is being developed.

National bibliographies

Bibliographie Nationale Française (http://bibliographienationale.bnf.fr)

This bibliography of legal deposit books catalogued since 1970 contains 1.3 million records and is now produced online by the BNF. It includes periodicals, government publications, electronic and donated materials from outside France.

French Canadian

The *Bibliographie du Québec* (www.bnquebec.ca), published monthly by the Bibliothèque Nationale du Québec in Montréal, lists all publications from Quebec province. Most if not all such publications are in French and the listing covers publications in French from elsewhere in Canada. From January 2003 the service is available exclusively online where it is updated on a monthly basis. Earlier print information is being added.

Titles in print services

Livres Disponibles (www.electre.com)

This French books-in-print service, available on the internet, covers French language material worldwide.

Livres Hebdo

A weekly service giving new title announcements, indispensable for up-to-date current coverage.

German

Materials in German are published in Germany, Austria and Switzerland, and in numbers of publications worldwide are second only to the English language output. In Switzerland a dialect version of German is also published. German library suppliers provide good online bibliographical information.

National library catalogue

Die Deutsche Bibliothek (*DDB*) (www.ddb.de/)

The German National Library catalogue online includes titles held in Frankfurt since 1945 and in Leipzig since 1974. This represents the unified Germany since 1990, and its unified national library on two sites, with holdings of some 16 million items. The Deutsche Musikarchiv in Berlin holds some 650,000 items of recorded music.

National bibliography

Deutsche Nationalbibliographie Aktuell

Includes items from the national libraries of Switzerland and Austria, and is published by the German National Library on CD-ROM. There are four series: 1945–1971, 1972–1985, 1986–1992 and 1993–1997.

Österreichische Bibliographie, known as the *OeB-online*
(http://bibliographie.onb.ac.at/biblio/)
This is the Austrian national bibliography.

Titles in print services

Verzeichnis Lieferbarer Bücher (www.buchhandel.de)
The German books-in-print service covers books, electronic materials, music, audio-cassettes, videos and software.

Karlsruher Virtueller Katalog (www.ubka.uni-karlsruhe.de/kvk.html)
This database allows cross-searching of major German, Swiss, Austrian, British and French catalogues, as well as some bookseller databases.

Spanish

Material in Spanish is published in Spain and in 18 countries in Latin America, most notably Argentina, Mexico, Chile and Colombia. Bibliographies for Spain are well established, while those for Latin America are less extensive, but there are several useful internet sites now available for checking details for orders. Spanish library suppliers, and internet booksellers for Latin America, are useful sources of current information. There is also a small amount of Spanish language publishing output in the Philippines and parts of North Africa.

National library catalogue

Biblioteca Nacional (www.bne.es/esp/cat-fra.htm)
The Spanish national library online catalogue *ARIADNA* is on the internet. This service aims to include all books catalogued since 1831 and will eventually include materials from the 15th century onwards.

National bibliography

Bibliografía Nacional Española
All books catalogued in the National Library of Spain from 1976 on CD-ROM.

Agencia Española del ISBN (www.mcu.es)
Books published in Spain since 1972, includes prices.

Titles in print services

Libros Españoles en Venta ISBN
This CD-ROM service for Spanish-language titles from 20 countries includes Catalan, Galician and Basque as well as translations into Spanish.

Spanishbooksinprint.com
This commercial service includes in-print, not yet published, audio, video and out-of-print titles in Spanish. There is a very useful Publisher Authority Database and access to tables of contents. This service can link directly to OCLC *Worldcat* if you need to check other libraries' holdings.

Italian

Italian bibliographies and catalogues tend to have considerable backlogs. The National Library is on two sites, in Florence and in Rome. Italian book suppliers can provide good online information on current publications.

Copyright deposit is made to the library in Florence, which is responsible for cataloguing the national collection, while the library in Rome catalogues foreign publications owned by the larger Italian libraries. The national library service, begun in the 1980s, works to improve co-operative cataloguing between libraries in Italy, with the aim of a national union catalogue.

National library catalogue

Biblioteca Nazionale Centrale di Firenze (www.bncf.firenze.sbn.it)
The national library catalogue is available online and includes the more than 600,000 items acquired since 1958. It is updated monthly.

National bibliography

Bibliografia Nazionale Italiana su CD-ROM
(www.alice.it/eb/catalogo/cdrom.htm)
This includes items catalogued since 1985, is available online or on CD-ROM, and contains information on books, serials, doctoral dissertations, children's books and music. This is one of the best resources for accurate bibliographical information.

Titles in print services

Catalogo dei Libri in Commercio (*ALICE*)
Italian books in print since 1989, available in three printed volumes – authors, titles, subjects – or on CD-ROM with monthly updates. An out-of-print CD-ROM service is also available.

Italian Books in Print (2002)
Commercial service.

Portuguese

Materials in Portuguese are published for the most part in Portugal and Brazil, Angola and Mozambique, as well as smaller countries in Africa. In Asia Goa and Macau also publish in Portuguese. The arrangement and overlap of bibliographies can be quite confusing.

National library catalogues

Biblioteca Nacional (www.bn.pt)

The Portuguese National Library catalogue can be accessed via the National Library website.

Brazilian Biblioteca Nacional (www.bn.br)

This website gives access to the Brazilian national library catalogue.

National bibliography

PORBASE (www.porbase.org)

PORBASE has served as the national bibliography for Portugal since 1988 when the print version ceased. It includes a small proportion (3%) of books from Brazil, and all legal deposit books from Portugal.

Bibliografia Nacional Portuguesa (http://bnp.bn.pt)

The Portuguese national bibliography can also be used online as a continuation from 2003 of the defunct paper version, or can be purchased on CD-ROM.

Titles in print services

The books-in-print service for Portugal entitled Livros Disponíveis was last supplemented in 2000.

British government publications

The whole area of official publishing has changed rapidly from print to electronic services, and as formats change, so too do the types of publication. Responses to consultation, or new series of statistics, may be more detailed on the web than they are in print. This is true of official reports in general, which if produced electronically are cheaper to mount on a website than to publish in print. The basic types of British government publications available both on the web and in print are: Bills, House of Commons papers, Acts, press notices, statistical tables, debates, Command Papers, Statutory Instruments, consultation and policy documents, and working papers. Some publications are now only appearing electronically, but paradoxically some reports and papers are becoming more difficult to trace in any form. It is often cheaper and quicker to download and print a document from a government website, than to order it as a printed publication.

Official sources of information

Traditionally, the publisher of British government publications was known as HMSO (Her/His Majesty's Stationery Office). However, in 1996 the trading business was sold and now operates as TSO (The Stationery Office) . There is a residuary body called HMSO with certain responsibilities which include:

- publishing Acts of Parliament and Statutory Instruments
- publishing measures of the Northern Ireland Assembly
- co-ordinating publication of Command Papers and some House of Commons numbered series
- administration of Crown and HMSO/TSO copyright
- maintaining the bibliographical record of government publications
- administration of the public library discount scheme.

From the HMSO website you can easily link to Parliament, the Scottish Parliament, the National Assembly for Wales (whose publications are promised to be totally electronic and bilingual) and the Northern Ireland Assembly. Since 2000 all UK legislation is published simultaneously on the internet and in print. The *Parliament* website provides information on publications from both Houses of Parliament in London. This site links to Select Committee reports and papers, and from the *Weekly Information Bulletin* and *Sessional Information Digest* there are links to green and white papers. Hansard is also available from this site.

TSO publishes for many Government departments and agencies, but also covers non-governmental public- and private-sector publishing. TSO publishes for the Scottish Parliament and the Northern Ireland Assembly, but not for the Welsh National Assembly. It does not publish for all official bodies in the UK, however. TSO is not only a publisher but also a sales agent for other bodies such as the BBC, and overseas official publishers such as the European Union, the United Nations and the World Bank. TSO has a network of UK bookshops and dealers who carry its stock, and offers a range of subscriptions and standing orders for the publications it handles. Another source of useful information here is the *Open Government* website, which covers public-sector information on a variety of topics.

The Stationery Office website provides links to its bookshop (www.tso.co.uk/ bookshop/), to general information and to other official bodies. It has been developing a more general *UK State* website, which supersedes some of the above, and you may find it useful. This includes the well known *Daily List* of government publications. The online bookshop is effectively a sales list, not really a bibliography, and therefore very useful for pre-order checking for acquisitions. You can search the site by title, author, description or ISBN, as well as by publication type. Similar but more detailed are the *Monthly List* and *Annual List* of government publications. The *Weekly Information Bulletin* and *Sessional Information Digest* are both excellent sources of information for tracing government publications. Each parliamentary session has its own index of papers from that session. Online ordering with a credit card is now a common method of acquisition.

Commercial services

UKOP Online (United Kingdom Official Publications) (www.ukop.co.uk)
This commercial subscription online guide to government publications in the UK, official, agency, unofficial and selected international publications, hosted by TSO since early 2003, combines The Stationery Office official catalogue and Chadwyck-Healey's Catalogue of British official publications not published by The Stationery Office. The catalogue, which is updated daily, goes back to 1980, and covers Parliament, the devolved administrations, Government departments, quangos, agencies and some international bodies such as the UN and World Health Organization (WHO). Subscribers have access to a considerable archive of full text material. E-mail alerts can be provided.

COBOP (Catalogue of British official publications not published by The Stationery Office)
A bimonthly microfilm service.

BOPCAS (British Official Publications Current Awareness Service) (www.bopcas.soton.ac.uk)
This current-awareness internet service, based on the holdings at Southampton University Library of British official publications since 1945, includes Government department and Parliamentary publications, white papers, green papers and House of Commons Library research papers. It provides abstracts, summaries and links. Basic bibliographic information for the last six months is

free, but all other services are on subscription. A second internet service called *BOPCRIS* (www.bopcris.ac.uk) provides digitized texts from 1688 onwards. It currently contains 24,000 references to key official publications up to 1995. There are abstracts and some full text provision.

Many government publications can be traced via the online catalogues of services with substantial collections of official publications, such as large academic libraries, as mentioned earlier in this chapter, as well as *BNB*. Most Government departments have their own information services, but although they are often willing to check items for the public, they are not always kept up to date about the publications of their own departments. Individual Government departments also have their own websites which are a good source of their publications. There are usually sections marked 'publications' and 'reports' and free downloads are often possible. The House of Commons Public Information Service is also helpful, as is the *Civil Service Yearbook*.

This very brief guide has only concerned itself with the UK, but of course the UK is part of the European Union and the EU's *Europa* website, with its links to the *Eurostat* service for European statistics, should be useful. The *European Information Association (EIA)* website is helpful too as well as *KnowEurope*. The latter is a paid service with some free elements, and has a useful directory of websites. For the USA you should use the excellent *GODORT* site as a starting point. GODORT is the Government Documents Round Table of the American Library Association. The *US Government Printing Office (USGPO)* access pages will provide an entry to their official publishing. Many large academic libraries in the USA are official repositories of USA national and state Government printing output, and official publications also appear in the catalogues of the Library of Congress. International bodies with useful websites for acquisitions include the UN and Organisation for Economic Cooperation and Development (OECD). Here you can download publications or make credit card purchases.

Music

Checking for materials about music is not really any different from checking other requests for purchase. Here the concern is to check for printed music and to an extent music recordings. Recorded music can now appear in a variety of formats: CD (compact disc), video, minidisc, DVD, and to a diminishing extent audio-cassette. DVD, which combines the sharpness and clarity of CD sound with digital video images, looks set to replace both video and audio-cassettes. Music can also be downloaded from the internet using the MP3 format, though a credit card is crucial. The MP3 internet site (www.mp3.com) claims to give access to more than 750,000 songs but it is only a streaming service. It is not set up to allow you to save sound files to a computer. This service is therefore much more suitable to individuals than to music collections. Printed music can also be downloaded from the web, and, by using specialized dealers, printed sheet music can be obtained from a website, with the musical key specified. If you do not order much in the way of music, then you can probably rely on your usual suppliers, but if you need a specialist supplier, look for advertisements in the professional press and do not ignore online bookstores.

Searching for printed sheet music and recordings really requires some knowledge of the subject matter, but an awareness of some important considerations can help:

1   Titles of works are often translated; for example, what is known in English as Stravinsky's *Rite of Spring*, will also be known as *Le Sacre du Printemps*.
2   Large works may contain several sections with individual titles.
3   Works occasionally have more than one title. Library users may quote shorthand names rather than, for example, the correct number of a symphony.
4   Opus numbers may be replaced by titles and vice versa.
5   Composers occasionally use pseudonyms or nicknames.

There is no real equivalent of any of the *Books in Print* series for music and it is important to have access to publishers' and dealers' catalogues to get price and availability information. There are now sheet music sites on the internet from which you can download material using a credit card. An example is the Boosey site (www.boosey.com). Such sites are set up by publishers, not aggregators, so you need to know the name of the publisher of the music you want before you can find it. In fact these sites do not usually offer instant downloading of sheet music, but just the opportunity to order online for postal delivery.

National bibliographies

British catalogue of music (BCM)

Published by Bowker, effectively the music score equivalent of the *British National Bibliography* (*BNB*) and includes:

- new music published in the UK
- foreign music purchased by the British Library.

It is arranged like the *BNB*, with a Dewey-classified section, a composer/title index and a subject index in the annual volumes. Information given includes: composer, instrument(s), title, place, publisher, date, opus or other index number.

Records are also accessible from the British Library via their online catalogue on the internet. The Library of Congress website also provides online access to music records via its catalogue.

Directories of music

The major historical listing of music manuscripts and printed music publications with locations of surviving copies is *RISM (Répertoire International des Sources Musicales)* or *International Inventory of Musical Sources*, which includes:

- Series A/1: a listing of printed music by individual composers published up to c. 1830, including locations of surviving copies.
- Series A/2: a listing of musical manuscripts, 1600 – c. 1850, available in electronic form only via the supplier NISC (National Information Services Corporation).
- Series B: a miscellaneous series including details of pre-1800 printed anthologies, details of music manuscripts up to 1600 and works on music theory.
- Series C: a directory of music research libraries which contribute to series A and B. You may prefer to use more general directories of libraries and specialist collections for basic information, as mentioned earlier in this chapter.

ISMNs

As already mentioned there are no commercial 'books in print' series for music; however, there are equivalents to ISBNs. Some modern printed music uses the International Standard Music Number (ISMN). This is a nine-digit number preceded by an M, but is not yet used by all music publishers. The final digit of an ISMN is a check digit, but is calculated in a different way from that of an ISBN. For this reason ISMNs cannot always be recorded in the ISBN field in an automated order system. They have been slow to catch on and the USA has only recently agreed to adopt them. For many music dealers it is anyway more important to record a catalogue number. For music recordings there is a system of ISRCs (International Standard Recording Codes) which can be applied to single tracks of music. However, this is not much used in music library collections. The *Music Publishers' International ISMN Directory* lists ISMN participating publishers by country with contact details and ISMN prefixes.

Commercial recordings listings

For the UK, RED (Retail Entertainment Data Publishing) is very useful (www.redpublishing.co.uk/) Their *musicmaster* database covers pop, classical, film and advertisement soundtracks and spoken-word materials currently available. It includes a comprehensive listing of UK distributors and other related companies. Individual record company websites provide recording samples, and the National Sound Archive is also a useful source for checking. Its catalogue is available via the British Library website.

Audiovisual materials

This section will look in outline at other sorts of audiovisual materials which you may have to order. Along with music, the most commonly ordered AV items for libraries are probably films, either as video or DVD for movies and audio, but audiovisual materials can also encompass audio-tapes, CD-ROMs, microform, computer software and items which turn out to be made up of several different media (sometimes known as kits). For those who are not used to handling this sort of material, there is sometimes a feeling that costs can be high, but that is not really the case, except perhaps for items like management training films, which are intended for corporate training budgets. Some AV material is available free, for example, from government departments, while some that is free from commercial companies is simply a prolonged advertisement. For public libraries, loans of music and films can be a welcome source of income, since customers are used to paying for loan from commercial outlets. There are, however, potential drawbacks in the medium itself. Videos, for example, are gradually being replaced by DVD, and may be more prone to damage than books. Vinyl records potentially keep better than audio-tapes, whereas CDs and DVDs currently have an unknown lifespan. Even CDs can be damaged or broken. AV collections have to keep up to date with both the message and the medium. The life expectancy of such materials depends on their storage once they have been acquired. As technology advances storage must include transferring older media such as open-reel tapes to cassette, or cassette to digital files, but this kind of operation is seldom the responsibility of acquisitions staff.

Format considerations

If your collection does not already have the kind of format you are being asked to order, there are several considerations to bear in mind before ordering, since much AV material cannot simply be placed on a shelf like a book. You must consider:

1 **Finance**
   Do you have the money to buy this kind of material?
   What are the costs of any software and hardware associated with the item?
2 **Equipment**
   What specialist equipment will be required?
   What service agreements are there for the equipment?
   Does the format you are buying work on the equipment you have?
3 **Use**
   What training will be needed for staff and users?
   Will the material be loanable?

Pre-order checking

There is very little in the way of official 'bibliographical' control of AV materials. Legal deposit of electronic materials at the time of preparing this book in early 2003 has just been agreed in the UK Parliament. Some of the European-language bibliographies described earlier in this chapter cover AV materials, as do the commercial books-in-print series described in Chapter 2. Few AV items have ISBNs, and there is a range of diverse publishers to deal with, including web publishers. There are published directories of various kinds such as *The Video Sourcebook*, but these tend to go out of date very quickly and will not always provide information about availability. Online web suppliers are another way to check details and availability of mainstream AV materials. Publishers' catalogues on the internet are the key guide for tracking down titles. *AV-Online* may also be helpful at the checking stage. *AV-Online* is a large database containing information on video, film and audio. Many titles which are no longer available (out of distribution, or 'OD') are listed. Also, by using the OCLC *First Search WorldCat* service in an advanced search mode, you can restrict searching to 'media', 'computer' or 'recording'. Cataloguing AV materials is fairly complex, so again a knowledge of cataloguing rules will help with pre-order checking.

Your usual suppliers should be able to handle AV but you may end up having to provide a good deal of the information yourself, unless the items you need are from major publishers. There is no real substitute for building up expertise in an area by the perusal of catalogues from specialist suppliers, and reading about the topic in specialist professional journals. Bookmarking relevant internet addresses is also important. For example, the BBC has useful information on its products on its website. The larger film studios also have good internet sites. Two websites which may help you identify movies are the enthusiastic *Internet Movie Database* and *Reel.com*. *FACETS* catalogue online is best for international cinema on video. There are some suggestions to get you started in the further reading items offered for this section.

Mention should be made here of the British Universities Film and Video Council, which provides subscriber services to UK higher education. Their website describes their library service, which stocks specialist journals and over 1000 international catalogues from producers and distributors of AV materials. Their *HERMES* database of AV materials and their index to broadcast television are both very useful, as they can provide copies under licence of television programmes. Their journal *Viewfinder* is useful for reviews, as is the American *Media Review Digest*. CHEST (Combined Higher Education Software Team) negotiate consortial deals on software for UK further and higher education, and maintain a useful guide to software products.

Alternatives to ordering

With AV material it is important not to be taken in by the novelty of the medium itself, since you need to check carefully whether what you are intending to order already exists in your collection in another format. Do not buy an online database which simply covers material you already have in print form, unless you are certain that there are advantages to having the material twice. Equally, electronic products from different publishers' bundles often overlap, and this will require careful checking. Do not assume that a video or DVD will be better for teaching purposes, when 35mm slides might give greater clarity for a complex topic. Do consider whether your institution is able to make licensed 'off-air' recordings from television, or borrow them from elsewhere rather than pay commercial prices. Copyright in this area is far from clear and you should take advice if you are in any doubt about the legality of stocking and lending such recordings. One example of the AV copyright minefield is the controversy over direct downloading of music from the internet. Some artists approve of this but recording companies are concerned about their commercial rights and lost revenue. Do take advantage of previews of material or trials, to ensure that what you are ordering is really what you want.

5
Suppliers

Choosing suppliers

Once a request for purchase has been thoroughly checked, and a decision made to place an order, the information can be passed on to ordering. Before ordering begins, however, there is a good deal of background work to be done. There is a need to weigh up various factors such as speed of supply, and balance them with variables such as price, accuracy and service from your suppliers.

Why choose a specialist library supplier?

It is possible to buy from a variety of sources but it is advisable first to consider those businesses known as library suppliers (vendors in the USA), who specialize in selling newly published materials to library and information services. Some of these suppliers may also have retail bookshops and/or hold stocks of materials for their customers. However, by no means all library suppliers are stockholders and you should not be unduly influenced by this attribute when choosing who to buy from. There are several reasons why you might want to use a specialist library supplier as opposed to, say, an ordinary retailer. The advantages of using a specialist supplier include:

1 **Efficiency**
   A supplier specializing in library supply should have good links with publishers, who do not handle single-copy orders with enthusiasm, and should be able to understand the needs of library services, taking a certain amount of bureaucracy off the shoulders of acquisitions.
2 **Financial advantages**, e.g.
   • discounts may be offered
   • delivery charges may be waived

- deposit accounts are possible
- pro-forma invoices can be avoided
- bank charges are lowered as invoices aggregate orders.

3 **Extra services**, e.g.
- access to bibliographic database
- processing (ownership labels, bar-codes, shelfmarks)
- binding
- catalogue records.

Considerations in choosing an individual supplier are given in more detail below. Some services are free to choose their own suppliers, but many have a loyalty to local dealers and, in the case of higher education institutions, to their campus bookshops. It is true that unless you have a very small materials budget you may be unwise to put all your eggs in one basket and only use one supplier. This could induce complacency and a deterioration in service from the supplier, or it could encourage higher discounts. Consortium purchasing, described below, is a way of filling some baskets with a lot of eggs and dropping others, by concentrating sales with just a few vendors. However, as library suppliers merge or disappear entirely, choices are actually becoming more limited anyway. Those that remain are shifting their role from that of book supplier to that of service provider.

How to find out about suppliers

There are some directories to help you find the names of suppliers. For international supply you can use the *International Literary Market Place*, which has the names of suppliers in many countries and general information on publishing. This does not mean, however, that your usual suppliers cannot handle overseas supply. For the UK you can use the Booksellers' Association website. This gives information on its members in the UK, with details of location, subject specialization and services. Only a small proportion of these will actually specialize in library supply. However, it can be a very useful directory if you need to buy something quickly in an area which you do not usually handle. You can also use *The Directory of Publishers* from Nielsen BookData. Unfortunately the rise of the larger book chains has seen some smaller bookstores merge or go out of business, so printed guides go rapidly out of date and it is usually better to use online services.

Apart from using directories you should scan the professional press for advertisements by suppliers. Check out suppliers' web pages but remember that these can be glorified advertisements. Make an effort to go to conferences and exhibitions so that you can make personal contact with suppliers, but also with other acquisitions staff who may well have useful opinions to give on suppliers.

Suppliers' information services

Suppliers of both new and second-hand material will send you catalogues and other information on request. The information may be in the form of e-mail alerts, or printed slips or cards for individual items. Alternatively it may take the form of substantial catalogues, some of which are not very easy to use. Some lists may cover materials on single topics or from only one country. Lists from review booksellers and from sales must be dealt with promptly but the other types of information should be circulated to the relevant interested parties, who select items for purchase. What information is sent to you will be decided by the completion of a profile form. Figure 5.1 shows an online form for setting up a profile with a supplier.

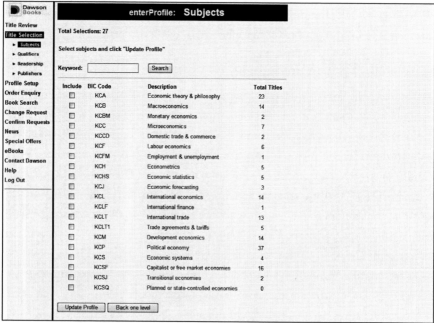

Figure 5.1   Setting up a subject profile with a supplier

Choosing the right suppliers

It may seem obvious, but in order to choose the right suppliers you need to know what your own requirements are. You also need to do some research on possible suppliers. The order in which you place various factors will depend on your own predetermined requirements. These requirements should be worked out by acquisitions in collaboration with cataloguing and reader services. For some, staff costs will be an important criterion as budgets decline; for others, service, and in particular servicing, will seem important as this delegates work to the supplier. Some will place greatest importance on data from the supplier's system, which may include an easy-to-use database. In the final analysis there will not be a perfect supplier to suit all your orders and you will have to compromise on some factors. What should not happen is that the supplier decides for you what your priorities are. Think first about what your users need most, and how acquisitions can serve them best.

Here are the major factors to think about while entering into discussions with potential suppliers:

1   **Customer service**
    Are there helpful staff who know what you are talking about?
    Is there a named contact for you?
    Will representatives call from time to time?
    How are customers kept up to date on developments?
    How are deliveries handled?
    Are they handled on a regular or more flexible basis?
    Are reports on non-delivery provided promptly?
    Is there an effective chasing system for outstanding orders?
    Can long-outstanding orders be automatically cancelled?
    Which other customers can provide references?
    Does the company participate in conferences and exhibitions?
2   **Financial matters**
    What is the financial health of the company?
    Is a discount offered on supply?
    When is a discount not offered?
    What is the frequency of invoicing?
    What information is included on invoices?

What are the terms of payment (e.g. 30 days credit)?

How will the invoices arrive: electronically, in parcels or separately?

How many copies of invoices are required?

Will invoices ever be in foreign currency, and if so how are exchange rates calculated?

Are separate invoices possible for separate budget funds?

Can invoices be paid electronically?

Are there handling/postage charges?

How are refunds handled?

How is tax calculated if it has to be paid?

If a price increases dramatically after ordering can the item be returned?

3   **Speed of supply**

What is the average arrival time for orders?

Can urgent orders be supplied more quickly?

Is there a personal contact for urgent orders?

Can you order online/by telephone/fax/e-mail?

Can orders be collected if necessary?

Are renewals of standing orders reviewed regularly?

4   **Automation**

Does the supplier have an automated system for customers? This might include:

- an online database for pre-order checking and ordering
- information on availability
- electronic order transmission
- claims
- electronic payment
- reports
- payment information and history.

Can the automated system interface with other systems? – e.g.

- the acquisitions system for information/transmitting orders
- the institutional finance system?
- publishers for transmitting orders/getting and giving information
- other services for obtaining information such as bibliographies of materials in print.

Does the system use standard approved protocols (e.g. EDI)?

5 **Range of supply**

Can material be supplied from non-commercial publishers?

Does the supplier have a specialism?

Does the supplier stock the kinds of material you will need?

What range of materials can be supplied (e.g. monographs, series, newspapers, government publications, foreign, e-books, microform, out-of-print, DVD)?

6 **Specialist services**

Is there an alerting service for new material (e.g. scanned title pages/printed catalogues/book reviews/illustrations)?

Are materials available on approval?

Are inspection copies available for academics?

Is a blanket order system available?

Can standing orders be supplied, including those for alternate years?

Can the supplier handle licences for electronic materials?

7 **Servicing**

What servicing can be carried out before delivery?

- physical processing
- lamination/binding
- fitting security triggers, ownership labels, barcode labels, date labels, spine labels.

Is cataloguing data supplied to agreed standards? And how?

8 **Problem-solving**

How do you return:

- faulty material?
- the wrong material?

How is credit handled for returns?

When are overdue orders chased?

How are cancellations handled?

How can an outstanding order be speeded up?

You must also consider your side of the bargain. What can you do to help the supplier send you materials in an efficient and timely manner? Suppliers need to know delivery and invoicing addresses.

Apart from using the directories mentioned, and the brochures that potential suppliers will be pleased to send you, contact with colleagues elsewhere can be very helpful, as can discussion of their experiences with different suppliers. Library suppliers should themselves be able to direct you towards other satisfied customers. You must consider your requirements carefully and convey them clearly to your chosen suppliers, or you will be unlikely to get the kind of service you want. It is impossible for any supplier, however experienced, to guess what the particular needs of your service might be. Equally, you cannot complain about poor service unless you have told a supplier what service you expect. It is very helpful if you can put your requirements in writing, along with a description of your ordering procedures and some sample orders. Your instructions to a supplier may not include as much detail as the points listed above, but you should have at least considered these before making an agreement. The record of your agreement should be kept on file, as should copies of any correspondence. Many suppliers will want you to fill in a customer profile form so that they can be sure that they have all the necessary information on your service. In any other kind of business you would sign a contract for supply, and you should view your agreements with suppliers to be a contract, however informal they may seem to be. When you have made an agreement with a supplier you will need to set them up on your order system, as Figure 5.2 shows. Preparing orders is described in Chapter 6.

Tendering for supply

Some services are obliged to put their materials supply out to tender. If this affects you, the checklist above will be a useful starting point in deciding what you need. The formal processes involved in tendering can be quite bureaucratic, but should not make you miss significant differences between suppliers. The processes you will be involved in are not substantially different from choosing a supplier on an individual basis. They are:

- identifying needs
- preparing a specification for supply
- selecting suppliers
- awarding contract(s)
- monitoring compliance with the contract
- reviewing and amending the contract.

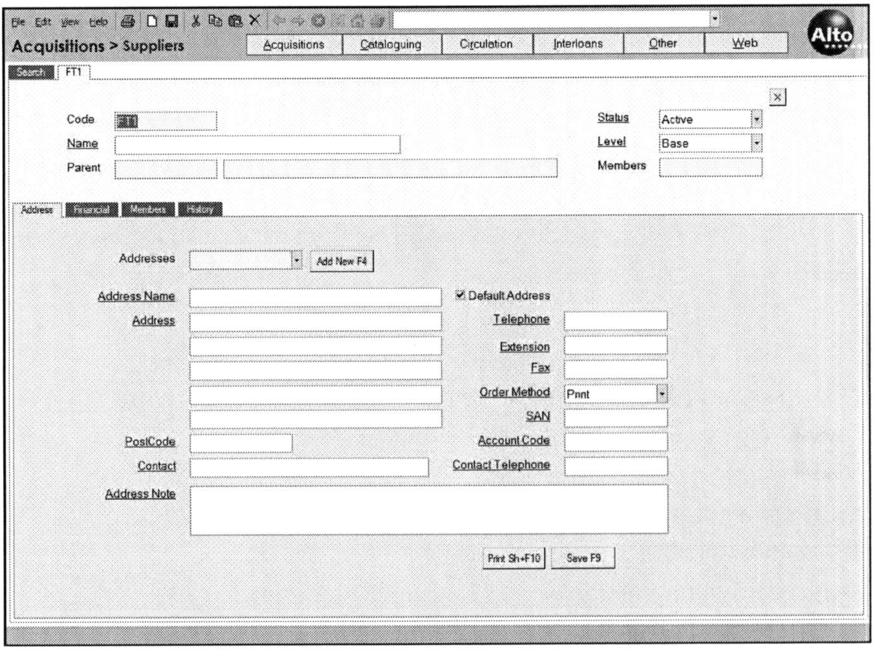

Figure 5.2 Setting up a new supplier on the order system

Outsourcing

One method of making the acquisitions budget go further is the increasing use of outsourcing – that is, passing some traditionally acquisitions-type work on to the supplier. Although some see this as a good way to contain costs, others claim that it represents a threat to professional expertise. What is certain is that, with continued advances in automation, acquisitions work is really changing, and it may be of advantage to pass residual clerical work to suppliers while retaining in-house what are known as core competencies. Outsourcing of some acquisitions activities may support a tendency to use a sole supplier, this being one way of ensuring continuity.

Activities which can be outsourced for acquisitions include:

- pre-order checking of details
- checking the existing order file/catalogue
- provision of management data on standing orders, discounts, etc.
- processing of materials (e.g. binding, bar coding, labelling, security tagging)
- negotiating licences for electronic materials.

Suppliers can also support collection development by selecting material and/or providing materials on approval. Suppliers and other companies such as OCLC working together can provide cataloguing data to agreed standards, and associated services such as classification. These services may speed materials to their destination more economically than employing technical services staff in-house.

To make the most of outsourcing any part of the acquisitions process you need to:

- calculate the costs of current in-house processes
- set this against the charges for outsourcing
- evaluate the likely effects of outsourcing
- investigate potential suppliers
- negotiate contracts
- monitor results
- keep up communications with the supplier
- recognize the effects on acquisitions and make needed changes to workflows.

Online e-services from suppliers

Just as the internet has become more important in acquisitions at the pre-order checking stage, so suppliers have begun to provide electronic resources to support the whole acquisitions process. In fact, supplier databases were available for order printing, claiming, fund accounting and access to bibliographical data before the internet became a widespread resource. Now, however, acquisitions can use online supplier services to economize on the effort previously put into checking a range of sources, including publishers' catalogues, as a logical extension to basic outsourcing.

It is not the intention of this book to cover collection development, but it is worth mentioning here that many suppliers now support selection by providing e-mail alerts, scanned title pages and covers, detailed content descriptions and links to reviews, along with cataloguing data, on online databases accessible to their customers.

Suppliers' databases can help acquisitions staff and selectors to verify order details. The same system can then be used to place orders electronically, and indeed be invoiced electronically. Databases can be used to create and check desiderata lists, and also to check the status and availability of current orders. The status report can form the basis for generating claims. Order records from supplier databases can generate catalogue records, speeding up the processing of new material when it arrives. Using these services can alter traditional acquisitions workflow and also tie you more closely to one supplier, or at least make it less attractive to move to a new one. You can use a supplier's database to create acquisitions reports, for example, on how many titles you have been supplied. Proper use of such a database can facilitate and speed communication between you and your supplier. It can also be generally more efficient since there is little or no re-keying of basic information. In some cases acquisitions staff are effectively missing out on pre-order checking entirely, relying on the supplier both for the bibliographic information and for discovering unintentional duplication.

Internet suppliers

Apart from specialist library suppliers providing access to databases and associated services, there is now a group of established online suppliers on the internet. Known as internet or web booksellers, these services, such as *Amazon.com*, market and sell books and other materials, including DVDs, cassettes, software and videos. They have extensive inventories, which are useful for pre-order checking and selection, and ordering online is easy. There is usually a capability for maintaining a personal subject profile so that you are alerted to new material each time you log on. Delivery times are given, and, although carriage charges can be high, it is possible to obtain books in 24 hours. However, they are not set up specifically for library supply, and you cannot therefore benefit from your usual negotiated discounts or servicing, nor will any order with such companies appear on your order system. Re-keying of order details by acquisitions staff will be necessary, and this may trouble auditors later. You will also need to use a credit card. On the plus side, delivery of material can be fast and the availability information is usually good and up to date. Some services now use internet suppliers at least to check pre-order information, if not to actually place orders.

Sitting, as it were, above these online bookstores are bookbots or shopbots such as *addall.com* and *bookfinder.com*, which can automatically compare book prices amongst major online bookstores, and which may help with discount prices. These services cover new and out-of-print materials, and also provide ordering facilities. Internet booksellers are particularly useful for urgent, secondhand and out-of-print orders, which are covered in Chapter 7.

Consortium purchasing

As acquisitions budgets are reduced, libraries and information services have looked at different ways of maximizing their money. One way of working towards more economical supply is for several services to work together in consortia. When operated well, a consortium can offer an organized approach to purchasing with agreed service contracts and discounts. It brings advantages not usually open to individual services. Initially consortia were set up for purchasing printed material but they are increasingly in operation for the purchase of electronic services, sometimes at a national level. Basically they are a means by which several local services band together, or rather buy together, to agreed contracts. Consortia are sometimes confined to particular types of libraries, although those for academic services are well developed, and there is increasing evidence of cross-sector consortia. More fully developed regionally in the USA, there are national consortia in the UK such as CURL (Consortium of University and Research Libraries) as well as several local consortia. Supranational consortia such as OCLC and RLG (Research Libraries Group) work across national boundaries, and there is an international coalition of library consortia called ICOLC.

Consortium deals are entered into for varying reasons. Cost is an important issue, as well as the potential for risk sharing in difficult markets, such as those for electronic services. Many libraries are obliged to go out to tender for their supply, and consortium membership can cut out much of the work needed to evaluate individual tenders. Equally, there are overarching imperatives such as the need for publicly funded organizations to follow nationally or regionally agreed purchasing guidelines, and to demonstrate transparency in their financial operations. The pooled purchasing power and experience of consortium members can allow a better approach to negotiation on prices, and certainly membership of a consortium which is purchasing electronic services provides what is likely to be wider access than an individual service could afford. There is more on finance in Chapter 9. Good negotiating skills and a knowledge of the current publishing and supply market are as crucial for consortium deals as they are for acquisitions in general.

For acquisitions there may be some perceived disadvantages to belonging to a consortium. A consortium deal can lead to a loss of local control over choice of supplier, added bureaucracy involved in negotiations, and an apparent additional workload when it comes to the evaluation of supply. Choosing which consortium to join might also be time-consuming. Some publishers are beginning to restrict the sale of electronic products to consortia only, and this can mean that acquisitions is tied to purchasing via a consortium at prices which may be no better than they could negotiate alone, and sometimes at prices which are unknown before supply. Finally, there is a distinct impact on the market as agents, suppliers and publishers vie to offer potentially untenable discounts, and we have definitely seen some suppliers disappearing because of this. Competition between consortia is also on the cards.

Ordering foreign material

When ordering materials from abroad you have at least three options. Pre-order checking is considered in Chapter 4. The first and least likely option is to make a direct order to the publisher. This could involve correspondence in a foreign language, payment in foreign currency, and delay. The second option is to order from your usual supplier, who will act as an importer, or direct from a specialist agent who handles the publications of overseas institutions.

The third option is to order from a supplier in the foreign country who will act as an exporter. You will have to use such a service if there are no selling rights in your own country. This is sometimes a problem for materials crossing the Atlantic. You can find out about such suppliers by scanning the professional press, attending exhibitions, or contacting an information or library service that you know specializes in this particular area. Some foreign governments will supply publications if you open a deposit account with them and keep up a certain credit rating. Some foreign exporter booksellers will supply both new and out-of-print materials. Online bookstores are also a good way to order foreign materials, and the French online dealers, for example, are very active in the new, second-hand and antiquarian markets. Online bookshops are useful for finding, tracking and completing information on elusive titles, particularly in foreign languages.

Evaluating suppliers

With the increased scrutiny of budgets from outside acquisitions, it is important to be sure that you are getting the best possible service from your suppliers. Service in this context covers the whole range of any agreement you have made with a supplier, as discussed earlier in this chapter. Monitoring that service from suppliers is important.

You may want to do a snapshot study, looking at one delivery of orders from your supplier, or one batch of orders going out to see what the results are. An automated acquisitions system can be helpful in providing data, though it seldom seems to be exactly the data we need. Colleagues in your service who deal with selection, cataloguing and reader services may have some firm views about your chosen suppliers, and these are worth investigating and documenting, with evidence rather than hearsay. You can use your automated system to check current statistics on your suppliers.

At the least you should think about checking up on your written agreement with your supplier, and consider the efficacy of the following factors in supply:

- new titles information/alerting service
- hit rate on supplier database
- average speed of supply
- urgent order service – average speed of supply
- delivery methods
- order status reports – frequent and accurate?
- claims
- number of items not supplied
- invoices
- prices and discounts
- servicing and materials processing
- customer service in case of need.

There are various reasons why you may want to check the performance of your suppliers:

- to support acquisitions in choosing new suppliers (is this a good supplier for you?)

- to confirm the suspected strengths and weaknesses of suppliers (are you sending them the right orders?)
- to reduce or increase the number of suppliers (is one supplier markedly different from another?)
- to change working practices in acquisitions (could more clerical work be passed to the suppliers?)
- to confirm or deny your own prejudices (we all think we know how a supplier performs but can we prove it?)
- to improve communication with suppliers (can you back up your comments with evidence?).

One of the themes of this book is communication, and if you go to the trouble of doing a survey on your suppliers and do not tell them the results, good or bad, you are wasting your time. Suppliers are not likely to improve unless you let them know where any problems lie. They are also under considerable pressure to perform, particularly in the context of consortia. If you talk to your suppliers, they will be able to tell you tales of how they were dropped without ceremony from one place, or of how another service complained about delivery times and then did not catalogue materials for over a year. In other words, you need to put your own house in order before rushing to criticize suppliers. A well thought-out and researched survey of performance, however, whatever the results, should do wonders for your relationship with your supplier.

6
Ordering

The format in which you send orders to suppliers can vary enormously, from a telephone call, fax, letter, marked-up information slip or e-mail, through to forms typed by staff, produced by your automated system, or purely electronic orders. Whichever method you choose, you will need to provide certain core information to the supplier and keep on file enough information for yourself, and most importantly to keep your users informed.

Information required by the supplier

The basic information required by a supplier in order to process an order with maximum efficiency is as follows:

- author
- title
- edition (if not the first)
- publisher
- ISBN
- price
- number of copies required
- format.

You will need to put this basic information onto your order system, as Figure 6.1 shows.

As has already been mentioned, acquisitions staff involved in checking requests for purchase need to know a good deal about cataloguing rules and practice. Increasingly, as order systems are automated, pre-order searching is online, and ordering involves editing a skeleton catalogue record. This record is

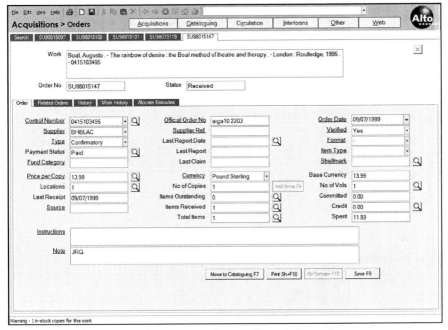

Figure 6.1   Order record on system showing basic information

then available for further editing when the order arrives. This has happened in manual systems too, where copy order slips are filed into the catalogue until orders arrive, or the order file is available publicly to users.

In any case it is good policy to edit order records to suit their eventual format in the catalogue. Using existing cataloguing rules to standardize headings will help users and staff to understand clearly what is on order when they check. Difficult headings such as those for official bodies will all be found together if the correct heading is chosen, and this should help to eliminate the ordering of unwanted duplicates.

A straightforward order, edited to accepted cataloguing rules, may therefore include:

- author
- title
- statement of responsibility, e.g. name of second or third author
- edition

- type or format of publication, e.g. DVD
- publisher (do not abbreviate: does OUP mean Oxford, Open, Osaka or Oregon University Press?)
- date of publication
- extent, e.g. number of volumes, discs
- notes
- ISBN
- price
- number of copies required.

For an order to send to a supplier, the statement of responsibility and any notes might be viewed as optional, but if the information is available and important to acquisitions at the order stage, it should be included.

The ISBN is crucial. The structure of ISBNs has already been explained in Chapter 3. An incorrect ISBN can easily elicit the wrong item, since publishers, their distributors and stockholding booksellers use these to pick books from stock. Take care over ISBNs for hardback and paperback bindings of the same text. If you always prefer the hardback edition, you should inform your suppliers as part of your 'Instructions to suppliers' which you agree when you first open an account. It can be helpful to put this information on your orders, but a wrong ISBN can override verbal instructions. If you want to order one paperback copy and one hardback copy, the simplest way is to make out separate orders. Automated order systems will be able to check the validity of an ISBN and reject the incorrect numbers which sometimes appear in information sources. For reasons explained in Chapter 4, order systems cannot usually validate ISMNs. If you are ordering from a catalogue, the item number from the catalogue and/or the date and code name of the catalogue should be included in your order.

Information required by acquisitions

The simple information which is sent to suppliers will not be enough for acquisitions purposes. When editing orders for input to your system, you will need to add other information. This could include some of the information which is already part of your purchase request form as described in Chapter 2 – for example:

- the requester's name and address/department
- instructions for routing the item on arrival to a special collection/particular branch
- reservation information for use on arrival
- the class or shelf number if this is already known.

Some of the information on classification will already exist if the order is for an added copy, replacement, new edition or continuation. If the order system has access to other databases from which you download records, you may also be able to find a class number if you use a standard classification scheme.

From time to time information has to be added to an order while it is in process. This may include notes about claims for outstanding orders, subsequent reservations, reports and supplementary information like a change of title. When any item is put on order, identifying codes can be added for in-house use:

- fund, branch or department to be charged
- supplier's name
- order date
- order number
- status, e.g. urgent
- authorization for order by responsible manager
- code for person inputting the order.

One of the many advantages of automated acquisitions is that this kind of information can to a large extent be added by default. Default suppliers can be set up to link with funds or subjects so that the system itself will allocate the supplier when it recognizes the correct fund code. So, for example, a specialist supplier for local studies material will be allocated by the system when it recognizes the local studies purchase fund code. Even if you are not able to allocate default suppliers but wish to make a judgement depending on the individual order, at least the names and addresses of suppliers used by acquisitions can be held on file, and called up by their own code when needed.

Once the supplier code is input at the order stage, the name of the supplier will appear in full on the order, and in the 'on order' file. The 'supplier' can also be listed as a donation or a direct order not made through the usual channels. Although your order system will be able to store the names and addresses of suppliers, as well as other information on them such as 'invoices in US $' it is still good practice to keep a comprehensive acquisitions address list with suppliers' names, addresses including mail, e-mail and URL, fax and telephone numbers. The name of your personal contact with the supplier is also important for queries. It is important to record contracts with suppliers and any collection profiles you have set up with them. Equally, if you correspond by e-mail with suppliers, you should keep this in a designated folder on your computer. These files should be regularly reviewed and backed up for safe keeping.

Once all the ordering information has been gathered together, it can begin to look rather complicated, and care must be taken to ensure:

- ease of pre-order checking for acquisitions
- ease of input to the order system
- that crucial order information is immediately obvious to the supplier
- ease of checking on receipt.

The way in which this prescription is followed in different services will vary considerably. Each information service or library adapts the ordering layout to suit its own specifications and those of its suppliers. It is a matter of regret that sometimes you have to adapt your order layout to one prescribed by your order system, but increasingly orders can be tailored to individual requirements. Acquisitions sections with few staff may need to send out orders with little detail, but this may cause delay in supply. It is almost superfluous to say that an order should be clearly marked 'ORDER', otherwise it will be ignored or shelved. This warning should also be heeded by suppliers, who may be ordering a publication from your institution.

Editing orders

Moving a request from pre-order checking to the point of actually sending off an order has been described so far as a rather mechanical process, but at various points along the way decisions will have to be made after the request has been checked.

If this is an added copy does the service need another?

The answer to this will depend on existing policy for multiple copy provision. For example you may need one copy for each branch of a public library service, or each site in an academic institution, or multiple copies for short loan sections. If it is decided not to order extra copies the requester should be informed that there is already a copy available.

Potential added copies can crop up frequently in the order process. The following list indicates the stages at which they may appear, with the reasons in parentheses.

- Catalogue check (already in stock)
- Order check (already on order)
- Circulation check (out on loan)
- Request form editing (forms appearing from different sources)
- Order input (ordered by someone else in the interim)
- Donation (failed to go through the above checks)
- 'Limbo' (arrived but delayed in processing)
- Supplier error (wrong item or order cancelled)
- Acquisitions error (inefficient checking)
- Reappearance of 'lost' item (user's conscience reappears).

Many of these problems can be avoided by ensuring that strict rules are adhered to in the creation of headings for orders. However, automated order systems do help the situation since they hold one record for both orders and catalogue and they can check automatically for unsuspected duplicates, as Figure 6.2 shows.

Which format should be ordered?

Once again the answer to this question will depend on policy. Format may mean the choice between hardback or paperback, or the choice of DVD or video, or the type of software required for a computer program. If you buy the wrong type of video you will find that it will not work on your equipment, but the considerations concerning hardback or paperback books are ones of price

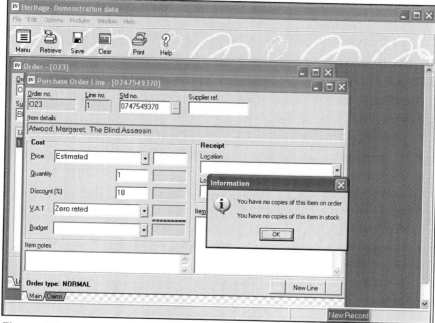

Figure 6.2   The order system checks for duplicates

and preservation. Paperbacks, particularly when they are partially rebound or laminated, are common since the price differential between the two types of binding is often so great that it is more cost-effective to buy two paperbacks than one hardback (and still have funds to spare). However, libraries which serve research and expect long-term use of their materials may prefer hardback for preservation reasons. The latter can withstand copying rather better.

Does the order need servicing?

Suppliers, as has been seen in Chapter 5, can provide servicing according to your specific requirements. The cost of these services is relatively low and effectively part of your discount. The decision on whether to use these services will depend on the availability of acquisitions or other staff to do these tasks, and on your policy on the purchase of different formats.

Which financial fund should the order be charged to?

Most services divide their budgets into separate sections. There is usually a general fund available for miscellaneous items. For public libraries the division is most likely to be by type of material, e.g. music, reference, local history, adult and children's materials. For special libraries the division of the budget may only exist if departments are being charged back for purchases. For academic libraries division will usually be by subject, although books, serials, AV and electronic may be separated. Some subject funds are effectively controlled by users, whose sanction is required for any orders on 'their' fund. If you are in doubt about the willingness of a fundholder to accept a purchase, you should refer back to the representative for the department. If the approach is refused and you still need to purchase the item, use the general fund. Budgets are discussed further in Chapter 9. Purchases can be split between funds, as Figure 6.3 shows.

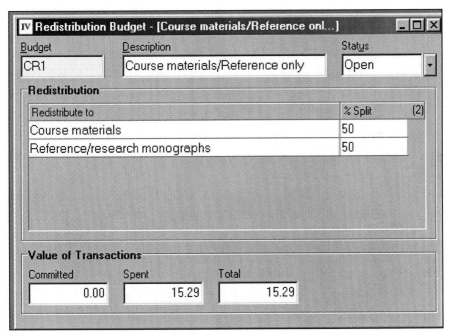

Figure 6.3 An order is split between two funds

Which supplier should be used?

The supplier to be used may be decided by the subject matter, language or the nature and format of the material to be ordered. As already mentioned above, a default supplier can be allocated, but it is unfair to direct only obscure orders to one supplier – they make little or no profit on these, and will not always give them their best attention.

Order input

Having made all these decisions, and edited the request to suit existing policy and rules, you can at last create an actual order. Whether this is done electronically or not, the result should be an order sent out, complete with order number and date, and an order file which is updated. In whatever way the order is recorded, you will need to be able to check it while it is out on order, perhaps either to chase it up or to ensure it gets special attention when it arrives.

If you are using a system which produces printed orders, you may want two copies of the printed order for your supplier, so that they can return one copy with the material, which will help you to pull up the record quickly that you need to check and 'arrive'. Pre-producing labels with suppliers' names and addresses can speed up the conventional mailing process, as can the use of window envelopes, so long as your system prints the address in exactly the right place and you have staff who enjoy origami. There is no point in completing pre-order checking and ordering quickly, and expecting materials to turn up quickly, unless you back this up by using first class mail for posted orders. Batching orders to send say, once a week may seem to maintain an even workflow, but is not guaranteed, nor should it be slavishly adhered to. Keep a record of how many orders are sent out in each batch, as this will be useful later on when the work of acquisitions is reported and recorded as described in Chapter 8.

Automated order systems

The major automated systems for library and information services all provide acquisitions modules. Some are, of course, better than others, and offer considerable integration with supplier systems. Interfaces with finance systems are developing or can be written as software enhancements. Automation came rather late to acquisitions compared to other parts of integrated library systems, and began rather as an add-on to cataloguing. Acquisitions staff were not always involved in the choice of systems and had to make do with what they were given. However, systems are improving as acquisitions has found its voice and has begun to impinge on the work of cataloguers by creating the record which will stick with the order, even if it is edited on arrival. If you are involved in choosing a new system, or modifying an existing one, here are some of the features you should look for. The ability of a system to combine several of the ordering processes on one screen improves the efficiency, speed and comfort of acquisitions staff.

1   **Order input file**

Records will display as part of a public information system/OPAC.

Records will include their status, e.g. on order, on approval, OP.

Staff access to the records will be more detailed than that for users.

Templates or order forms can include pre-set defaults, e.g. 1 copy.

Records will be searchable by several keys, including order no, date, author, title, ISBN.

Duplication checking and warning capability.

Automatic allocation of order numbers.

A potential for adding subsequent notes, e.g. reservation.

2   **Supplier file**

Names and contact details are held, with keyword access.

The file can be called into play by default for certain funds/formats.

Default values may be pre-set for: discount, currency, automatic claim period.

It should be possible to add items with no order, e.g. donations, exchanges.

3   **Output**

Orders/e-mail/EDI

Addresses for receipt/payment automatically added to orders

Claims at pre-arranged and random times

Cancellations

Orders awaiting verification

Routing or circulation information on arrival.

4   **Accounting**

Electronic invoicing

Committed (encumbered) figures calculated for items on order

Expenditure figures calculated for items arrived and paid for

Separate fund accounting

Payment history for individual orders

Charge-back accounting capability

End-of-year accounting

Currency conversion

Audit trails

Interface with institutional finance system.

5 **Management statistics**

Number of items on order, received, paid, claimed, cancelled

Performance data on individual suppliers, e.g. average delivery times, discount, number of claims required

Average prices

Performance data on separate funds, e.g. percentage of budget spend.

System suppliers are in business to make money, and to do this they work to improve their products. Acquisitions staff should make their voice heard in the choice of system and in the priority order for enhancements and upgrades.

EDI

EDI (Electronic Data Interchange) is a cross-domain standard by which orders/information are transmitted and acknowledged electronically between library services and suppliers, and onward to publishers, distributors and wholesalers. While it was relatively slow to take hold, much of the public library community now uses EDI for processing acquisitions, and it has gained acceptance with academic institutions and publishers too. All the major library system suppliers support EDI and will set up supplier links for acquisitions. Data is imported automatically into the order system, and can be exported into your finance system. This electronic exchange of information between different systems is known as interoperability. All the major library suppliers offer EDI facilities. EDIFACT comprises the international rules for the use of EDI, which is used generally for e-commerce, not just library and information service supply.

The potential advantages of using electronic ordering can be seen as:

- electronic information pre-ordering/quotes
- improved accuracy in orders (no rekeying of data)
- speedier processing (no waiting for letters to arrive)
- reduced overheads (staff, postage, paper and printing)

- speedier supply
- electronic invoicing
- less use/filing of paper records
- the supplier may offer higher discount if EDI is used
- internal acquisitions processes are streamlined.

EDI supports a variety of useful standard messages, not all of which are available on all systems. The format of messages is standardized in the UK by Book Industry Communication (BIC) and development work is converging with that in the USA on a new standard called ONIX. Possible messages include:

- orders
- quotes, used for:
    - selection from showroom visits
    - supplier selection
    - supplier database selection tools
- acknowledgments for reporting purposes, e.g. price changes
- invoices
- fulfilments – connecting acquisitions with cataloguing
- claims.

Logical developments in the use of EDI may prompt automatic orders when a library circulation system shows that it needs more copies of a particular title, or indeed a library user prompts an order via the OPAC. One possible disadvantage of using EDI is that it ties you to those partners in supply: system suppliers, materials suppliers and publishers who support the use of EDI. Some consortial deals demand the use of EDI. It also denies in some ways the open standards of e-commerce on the internet, which allow you range and choice. Having said that, the internet can encourage the whimsical, almost unintentional, ordering of material. Naturally, acquisitions is never whimsical in its ordering of materials.

7

Out-of-the-ordinary ordering

Once a good relationship has been established with suppliers, routine ordering should not cause too many problems. However, you will sometimes need to buy materials which take more time and patience to pursue. The internet has provided acquisitions with some interesting solutions to what were previously problems.

Urgent orders

Part of your arrangements or contract with suppliers should include an agreement on how urgent orders will be handled. Some suppliers have a ready-made system set up for dealing with urgent orders. The most common method of coping with this is to telephone, fax or e-mail the suppliers with order details. They will in turn contact the publisher, who will send the item directly to you if necessary. The invoice will follow later from your supplier. This is usually a good way to get a fast response, so long as you have previously set up the mechanism with your supplier. An even quicker way is to buy the material over the counter. However, unless the retailer is one of your usual suppliers, you will not receive the discount to which you are normally entitled. You may also face payment problems, since you will not be able to pay on account. If you are likely to use this method, then be sure that acquisitions has enough petty cash available or that a simple method of reimbursement is available. Be sure to keep careful records of all such orders.

Online urgent orders

An increasingly successful method of dealing with urgent orders is to use an online internet dealer or bookseller as described in Chapter 5. The benefits of this kind of e-commerce are:

1   **Speed of supply**: if the internet dealer has the item in stock, you really can get it the next day.
2   **Stockholding**: some of these suppliers will have a broader stock than you can find close to home.
3   **Ease of ordering**: you do not need to leave your desk to place an order.

The disadvantages of this kind of order are:

1   **Payment**: a credit card is usually needed (see Chapter 9).
2   **Security**: security of credit card details is not always guaranteed.
3   **Discount**: there is not usually a discount as with your normal supplier.
4   **Postage**: there are significant carriage costs
5   **Servicing**: materials will need servicing in-house.
6   **Order files**: there is no link to your order system, so information must be re-keyed.
7   **Audit**: the audit trail is unusual (see Chapter 9).

Why the rush?

There are further pitfalls in urgent orders, known as 'rush' in the USA. Although the item may indeed be urgently required, it must not miss any of the normal pre-order checks. It is quite possible that the title is already on order or in stock. If it is already in stock, you can inform the requester, and fetch or reserve the item for them. If it is already on order, you can chase the supplier urgently. Pre-order details should still be checked since a high price could preclude purchase. The discovery that the urgent item is out of print, or not yet published, would involve informing the requester of a possible delay. At worst, checking may reveal that you have the wrong details on the request, which should make the checking return to square one.

Finally, in the light of experience, you will have to decide whether a request marked urgent really is urgent. A batch of 30 requests, all marked urgent, are unlikely to be all equally urgent; and anyway, treating them all as urgent will slow up the normal requests. In a special library a higher proportion of items are likely to be urgent, and will need to be purchased rapidly. You will also get to know by experience which suppliers and publishers are able to handle urgent orders, and when you will need to order direct. You should of course record the urgency on your order system, so that the item is dealt with quickly once it arrives. Your users, who will probably have become used to the speed associated with web ordering for themselves, may need careful explanations if you cannot fulfil their request immediately.

Direct orders

Direct orders are those sent directly to the publisher, bypassing the normal supplier. These will usually be for non-trade publications, i.e. publications which do not come from the large commercial publishing companies. The most common sources are professional associations, academic institutions and private individuals, who act as both the publisher and supplier of their work. Locating such a source on the internet and verifying details, and perhaps placing a direct order there, or at least sending an exploratory e-mail, will speed things up. One site which might help is the University of Waterloo, Canada, *Scholarly Societies Project*, which provides information and links to scholarly societies worldwide. For acquisitions units with few staff, your normal supplier will have to suffice for these materials. This will, however, impose a delay, and possibly a handling charge. There is unlikely to be any discount allowed. It is not good practice only to give this kind of more difficult request to one supplier. For the best service, non-commercial orders should be interspersed with substantial commercial ones.

Advantages of direct orders

The major advantage of a direct order is speed. Orders sent from small institutions or private individuals can come very quickly. If you are able to contact them personally, orders can be sent out the same day. Some commercial publishers encourage direct orders, particularly pre-publication orders, and this can provide a substantial discount on the published price. These discounts are usually made on large works such as a new multivolume encyclopaedia or dictionary. You may be obliged to commit yourself to purchase well before publication, and depending on what stage you are at in the financial year, this may not be possible. Sometimes pre-publication offers look like 'testing the market', but publishers always deny this. Be sure to check whether any pre-publication offer will actually improve on your usual supplier discount, and if so, whether your usual supplier can match the price, thus saving you extra work.

Disadvantages of direct orders

The major disadvantages of direct orders are checking for details before ordering and the handling of payment. Many smaller non-commercial publishers do not issue anything but the flimsiest of publicity, and you may have to spend some time verifying authors, titles and prices, and finding out addresses. If you are not able to trace enough information, an e-mail or a telephone call to the institution, or to another collection which specializes in this kind of information, or checking their catalogue online, should provide some of the answers you need. Make a note of any useful names and addresses as future contacts.

Payment for direct orders is often in the form of cash with order (CWO) or credit-card payments. If you know the price of the publication it is better to pay up front or you risk receiving a pro-forma invoice, with all the delay that entails (see Chapter 9), rather than the item you want. An order from acquisitions might in this case get no response unless it includes payment. Direct orders abroad, particularly those requiring pre-payment, are not recommended unless you are sure of the source. Some direct orders will be free but you might still be charged postage costs. Some smaller suppliers might want you to open an account with them and many large publishers refuse small direct orders below a certain value.

Standing orders and continuations

Most information and library services have some standing or continuations orders, although they are not always the province of acquisitions, since they can tie in more closely with procedures for buying journals or serials. If these orders are handled by separate departments, care must be taken to liaise between the two to avoid duplication of orders, especially since some titles carry both an ISSN and an ISBN.

The term 'standing' order means that you expect to receive successive titles in an ongoing series until the standing order is cancelled or the series ends. This might be:

- all volumes in a numbered (or un-numbered) series
- all works by a particular composer in a series
- all official publications from a government department

- all proceedings of a regular conference/lecture series
- all annual volumes of a reference work.

It is crucial to keep very careful records of standing orders, and for your supplier to check regularly that orders are being fulfilled. Always record standing orders on your order system. Some publishers will not accept direct standing orders, either from you or from your suppliers. In this case, publicity material can be used to check when a new volume is available, but you can still ask your supplier to do this for you. Figure 7.1 shows an enquiry being made of a supplier system to check on an outstanding standing order.

Subscription agents or serials suppliers will also handle standing orders for you. They have more expertise overall in handling irregular series, as well as annuals and conference proceedings. They are also more likely to be able to handle the purchase of publications which require membership of the issuing organization. They can offer some processing, as do monograph suppliers. Serials or subscription agents maintain substantial databases of serial titles, which are available to customers online, and decreasingly in print. These can support your pre-order searching for standing order titles. Series can also be

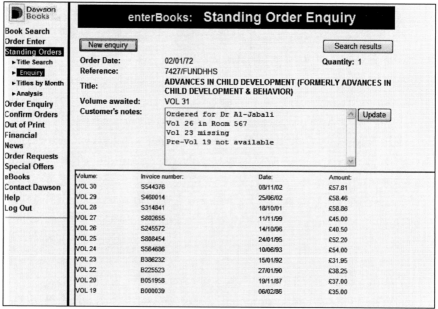

Figure 7.1   Checking the status of standing orders with supplier

checked via your usual supplier database and they can include series in your profile for any alerting service. Your suppliers' ongoing relationships with publishers mean that they can treat some items as standing orders on your behalf, even if the publisher will not recognize them as such. Standing orders represent a substantial financial commitment and their acquisition and use should be reviewed from time to time, just like serial titles. For specialist standing orders such as loose-leaf legal materials you should use a specialist supplier.

Blanket or open orders

Blanket orders are much like standing orders. They may be placed with publishers or your usual suppliers to provide, for example, the whole output of a specialist supplier. In the case of small institutional publishers it may be necessary to pay an annual membership fee as well. Such an order might provide, for example, everything that the United Nations publishes on Africa but not on Asia. Blanket orders therefore have a slightly less certain outcome than standing orders, in that the number of possible publications is infinite. Discounts on blanket orders can be very good, as the publisher has guaranteed sales. Once a blanket order is placed, you are committed to accepting and paying for the material received until the blanket order is cancelled. Since the financial outcome is very unsure, great care must be taken before you commit yourself to a blanket order, and you should monitor costs and use.

Material on trial

Approvals

The term 'on approval' has two different meanings in acquisitions work. The first meaning is getting individual titles on approval to look at and to check. If you are unsure about the wisdom of ordering a title, you can make use of 'on approval' services available from many publishers and suppliers. They are sometimes known as 'see safe' in the trade, although this may further imply to a supplier that if they obtain materials on approval from a publisher, they will either purchase these or items to a similar value. But for acquisitions the term 'on approval' means a 'sale or return' policy.

Titles you request in the first sense of 'on approval' can be held for a period of around two to three months. If you decide to buy, you can pay on the invoice which accompanies the material. On-approval copies should be retained in acquisitions for inspection, since they are your responsibility. They should also be kept in good condition, so that if you decide to return them the supplier will be able to resell them. Approval items can be recorded on the order system for users to see, and allocated to a budget. Figure 7.2 shows allocation to funds on the order system.

The second meaning of approvals, more commonly known in the USA as approval plans, is a much larger enterprise altogether. With approval plans a library or information service will contract with a supplier, or less commonly a publisher, to provide regular deliveries of material on approval, from which selectors will choose those titles to be purchased. There will be an agreed profile drawn up. This is one step away from e-mail alerts and notification slips mentioned in Chapter 5, but these may also be used as part of an approval plan, as can electronic notification to acquisitions. In fact detailed e-mail alerts with substantial descriptions of books may overtake the usual kind of approval plan, with choices being made without seeing the physical items.

Approval plan profiles can be drawn up to cover, for example:

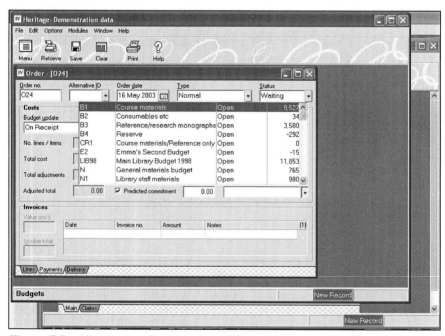

Figure 7.2 Allocation to funds on the order system

- all titles from a single publisher
- all titles from a range of nominated publishers to cover agreed subjects
- only materials suitable for a particular level of user
- all titles from or about a particular country or area
- all materials of a particular type, e.g. classical music CDs
- all titles in a particular subject area.

Approval plans are one version of outsourcing, or at least one step along that road. Suppliers with substantial approval plan services employ professional selectors to identify and acquire the correct materials for their customers. It takes some responsibility and work away from acquisitions while giving the supplier an assured income. Care must be taken not to duplicate standing orders or blanket orders. Checking on such duplication can be done by your supplier.

Since most material provided in this way is newly published, and approval plan suppliers can also service the materials, this can also speed up the process of acquisitions. Professional staff in the various subject areas select from deliveries, or increasingly from a database, what they need to buy, and unwanted material is returned. While discounts on approval plans may be considerable, the items purchased can also be a substantial drain on the acquisitions budget and a minimum spend may be part of the deal. Enhanced supplier services, such as access to descriptive database entries which can show what you already have on order, can help to keep the agreed profile active and relevant to your service. Suppliers can also provide financial data on costs to date and projected expenditure.

If you decide to have an approval plan, you will want to monitor how it works, not only from a financial point of view, but also, more importantly, from your users' point of view. Features to check include:

- prompt delivery of new publications / information
- correct publishers, subjects, level covered
- success in getting the material you want
- minimum duplication with other orders
- ease of use of supplier database
- usefulness of financial data

- quality of information provided
- ability to tweak the approvals profile effectively.

Inspection or examination copies

Academic staff, or specialists in a subject, often request, or are sent on approval, copies of newly published work in their field. These are known to teachers and lecturers as inspection copies. Publishers send them with the added incentive that if they are subsequently adopted as a course text, and therefore recommended to groups of students, the preliminary inspection copy will not be invoiced. They are often retained until it is too late to return them, and at this point the lecturer concerned may try to persuade acquisitions to take them on complete with their overdue invoice. If you are normally entitled to a discount, you have a perfect justification for refusing this type of material. By the same token, approval copies are more economically handled via your normal suppliers. If necessary a supplier can give a price quotation before supply, if that is the feature of an order which particularly concerns you. Inspection copies of serials are a simple but often slow way to check whether a recommended new purchase is really needed.

Showroom and supplier visits

Some suppliers encourage acquisitions staff to visit either special stock showrooms or their own retail stores. Such visits may coincide with the end of the financial year if there is still some money in the budget, or they may be used to pick stock to build up a new or neglected area. Some suppliers set up specialist exhibitions for particular needs such as school libraries. Suppliers' automated systems can be used to good effect to collate the necessary information and send either invoices or quotes which allow returns.

Electronic materials

Electronic materials are burgeoning and provide particular challenges for acquisitions. Oddly enough, publicity for such materials as databases, DVD, specialized software and web-based services often appears in glossy printed form. You will need to do a good deal of investigation before ordering to establish the following:

- the product name
- the publisher
- available formats
- the URL for product information
- parallel products (is this already available, for example, in print or free on the internet?)
- bundling (is this material already covered in another product, and if so to what extent?)
- user authorizations required (e.g. IP address, password, restrictions to n users, common access password)
- licensing and networking (number of users possible at what cost over what area, and is any legal advice needed?)
- any additional ICT equipment required
- trial possibilities and conditions
- evaluation results from other users
- availability through co-operative/consortium purchasing
- user training required
- customer support available.

Many electronic products can be handled through your usual book or serial suppliers, but you should if possible arrange a trial covering different formats. The CD-ROM version of a database may be good and well tested, but a newer web subscription may not yet be fully developed, or provide the kind of continuous multi-user access that your service needs.

Some of this may seem rather negative, and when you get to the question of price, there is a good deal of investigation and negotiation to do. To look on the positive side, electronic products do have substantial advantages over print. Electronic services can be kept up to date more easily and can be subjected to detailed searches with comparative ease. They can provide you with reports on the frequency of use and they can save wear and tear on valuable printed items. What is not yet proven is how long the various electronic formats and their associated equipment will last and indeed be archived. Audiovisual materials are also considered in Chapter 4.

E-books

There are two types of e-books at the moment, those which represent an e-version of a whole book and those which are effectively databases of linked materials. No very good definition of an e-book exists but the closest at the present time might be a combination of electronic reference works, monographs and textbooks. They can be delivered via the web to a user's computer or to specialized hand-held devices (e-book readers) or other hand-held devices such as palm pilots. The obvious advantages for users are access at any time and any place, combined with the freedom to search and manipulate a complete text online. First-time purchase of e-books nearly always implies specialist software too.

Students appear to be the major customers for e-books, partly because they are already so used to taking digital material such as music and movies from the internet, as well as e-mail. A major use of e-books is high-use student textbooks, and recent surveys show that economics, business, computing and medicine texts are proving popular and well used. Of course, electronic delivery of such material means that good data on use can be provided, unlike the use of conventional books in libraries which cannot be measured effectively.

Considerations for acquisitions include the current availability of titles, and the lack of good consistent information about availability. E-books began as something akin to reprints, providing titles from publishers' backlists, but there is now far more activity from the current frontlist. A mixture of old and new material is being produced electronically by some publishers, of which Oxford Reference Online and Oxford Scholarship Online are prime examples. A substantial publisher's output should ensure quality, but there are still questions to consider in the realm of distribution and licensing, and also printing models. Publishers' catalogues and websites now show whether or not titles are available electronically. Evaluation of different suppliers of e-books, in terms of quality, depth and timeliness, is under discussion. Managing e-books from different sources requires extra work.

E-books are currently in a relatively early stage of development, just as library and information holdings are becoming hybrid, with a mixture of print and electronic materials being acquired. It seems likely that e-books will ultimately evolve into something rather different from printed books – the analogy of TV and movies is perhaps applicable in this context. In this transitional stage of development, intermediary companies promoting and supplying e-books come and go with alacrity. The most stable at this time seems to be *NetLibrary* but even this has been taken over by OCLC, which has meant changes, if only in pricing models. These companies negotiate with publishers to digitize their titles and sell them on with a licence. Consortial deals are also made for e-book collections or selections. Secure technology protects the publisher's copyright. Some usage controls and conventions are currently library-bound, for example only allowing one user at a time. In the field of modern fiction some titles are now being published only on the web, with a charge made for access.

E-books imply a change in our relationships with publishers on the one hand, and users on the other. Acquisitions work, which has previously been squeezed by serial price hikes, will now need to consider budgets for e-books, particularly as many titles, like electronic serials, will be electronic versions of titles already held in print, but still required by readers. A curious feature of e-books may be that, while they are paid for by libraries, they will not actually be owned by them.

Out-of-print and second-hand material

Out-of-print material

The quest for out-of-print and second-hand material used to imply a search for material which was definitely old, but nowadays it is not unusual for a new title to go out of print within a matter of months, and for acquisitions to be searching for it soon after that. Much of the out-of-print material you need may only be available on the second-hand market, but there are some reprint series, microform or on-demand reprinting services which may suit your purposes.

Any requests which you discover to be out of print, either at the pre-order stage or when this is reported to you by your supplier, should be marked so that you can create a list, sometimes known as a 'desiderata list' or 'wants list'. Items in this category can be reviewed from time to time to ensure that they are still needed, and information kept on when they were reported as being out of print. When an OP or Out of Stock report is received, be sure to check with the requester that the material is still needed, or whether it can be removed from your files. The desiderata list can be sent to dealers, and you can ask for price quotations on any titles which are available. If your usual in-print supplier has reported a title out of print, even though it was only recently published, a direct call to the publisher's warehouse can sometimes elicit a few copies of an elusive title which may have been declared out of print a little prematurely. This sometimes happens because a new edition is in preparation.

Second-hand material

A good relationship with second-hand dealers in your field can help with tracing such materials. You can set up a subject profile much as you would with in-print suppliers. You can also agree price and condition ranges that you are prepared to accept. Again, quotations before supply are possible, but bear in mind that mark-ups on original prices can be high.

It is important to realize that many second-hand dealers do not have shops as such, but operate from home and almost exclusively by mail and e-mail. Scanning the catalogues of second-hand dealers can be useful, but it is very time-consuming and staff may not have the time to do it well. The internet is helping to save time here, as dealers set up their own websites. However, you should remember that anyone can set up a bookshop on the internet, and not all such sites provide the kind of professional services acquisitions staff might need.

OP on the internet

The internet has radically improved the task of locating and purchasing out-of-print material, and has become a crucial resource. For recently out-of-print modern material, useful information can be found via the online internet booksellers which specialize in new materials. However, if you have a substantial desiderata list, one method of sourcing supply is to post the list on an aggregator or bookbot internet service, which will make searches and provide price quotations for you. To check details you can use the listing services mentioned for new titles in Chapter 2, since these also cover out-of-print materials. If you are making internet searches yourself, you can use *AcqWeb* to find a list of suitable websites. Many, but by no means all, of the sites are USA-based. Some of the sites most commonly used include *Advanced book exchange* and *half.com. Bookfinder.com*, as described in Chapter 5, is a bookbot on the web, which searches across several dealers' sites to find different prices and locations.

There are many others, and new ones often appear as old ones disappear. *AcqWeb* will keep you up to date on new services, including foreign sites, which you may want to try. Generally speaking, suppliers of out-of-print items on the web do not charge you for making a search, just for the material itself. Costs are paid for by the dealer posting their information on the web, or by the use of online advertisements. Some services can deal with orders and invoices, while others will need credit-card payments. Generally invoices are handled by the aggregating service if one is used, and not by the individual dealers which they represent.

One of the fortunate side effects of OP e-commerce is that prices have tended to come down. Previously you might only have found one copy of an OP item via a printed catalogue. Now you may find several different copies in varying conditions and with varying prices, and you and the dealers are comparing prices. Specialist dealers who know what the profile of your service is can now alert you by e-mail to potential items for purchase.

There are important national websites which have taken over from published guides to dealers. One such in the UK is the *Bookworld* site, which acts as an agent for dealers, private collectors and libraries wishing to sell old, rare, scholarly and OP materials. They also deal in new items from small publishers.

There are still plenty of second-hand dealers with shops to browse, but it's all a matter of what time you have to spare, compared with a quick internet search and a speedy response providing several choices.

Book sales and auctions

Book sales organized by publishers or dealers can be a good way of buying, for example, reduced-price hardback books, or building up a new or weak stock area, or replacing missing or stolen items, or adding extra copies of busy material. You should not overlook the fact that this material is on sale because it is unwanted, outdated or damaged.

Second-hand or antiquarian book sales are where you can find specialist dealers displaying their wares, often at high prices, but it can be useful to actually handle the goods and strike a bargain. Auction sales can be either extremely specialist or rather miscellaneous, and in either case they can be very time-consuming. In the first case you may pay high prices for one item, while in the second you may pay for a box of items only a few of which you need. There is no real substitute for viewing such material before a sale and making a note of a ceiling price beyond which you would not bid for any lot. Bidding can be fascinating and addictive, and is now also available on the internet, where the same caveats apply.

Remainder and review dealers

Both remainder and review dealers handle relatively recently published material. This kind of stock can also be found in regular bookshops and on the internet. Remainder dealers handle bulk stocks which publishers want to sell off quickly, whether because the title is not selling well, is being revised, or is taking up valuable warehouse space. Discounts of up to 30% are obtainable.

Review dealers handle titles which have been sold on by reviewers or reviewing journals. They may or may not have actually been reviewed, but are often very up to date. Some of these dealers specialize in certain subject areas and can list available items, but turnover can be quick so you need to act expediently. Again discounts of around 30% can be had, and it is sometimes a good way to buy a cheaper casebound book which you could otherwise only afford in paperback.

Using these sorts of dealers will involve you in looking at opportunity costs. Balance the speed of supply and discount you receive against the uncertainty and irregularity of supply. You may not get the order you want, and even if you do, you will have to load up orders on your system from scratch. There will be no servicing available.

Reprints

Reprints of out-of-print materials are often expensive. However, they can bring together widely scattered works, or those so long out of print that you would be unable to get them in any other way. They should also be in good condition compared to books from second-hand dealers. Reprints are sometimes announced to test the market, and if sufficient orders are not forthcoming the reprint may not appear. Reprints are not always in book format and can be microform, CD-ROM or online databases. Some can be traced via the *Guide to Reprints* (2003) and you can use *AcqWeb* to find other sources.

Some publishers will provide on-demand reprints of OP titles, but these can be expensive. There is no doubt that larger publishers are beginning to recognize the value of their backlist material. The development of digital printers makes commercial reprints with low volume print-runs much more economically viable, even for single copies. There are quite a few internet services offering reprints to order of individual books. An example is *Lightning Source*. If you really cannot locate an OP title to buy, it is sometimes possible to persuade individual publishers to agree to your making a complete copy of a title which you can borrow on interlibrary loan. Finally, the existence, or possibility of ordering, microform versions of what you are looking for should not be overlooked. The *International Guide to Microform Masters*, which is compiled from the catalogues of over 200 libraries in the USA and Europe, has more than 1.4 million possibilities in microform described. The *Guide to Microforms in Print* (2003) lists 166,000 publications available in microform.

There is no such thing as a free book

It is actually sometimes possible to receive publications free of charge. This can apply to reports from government and other official and unofficial bodies. However, fundamentally they are not free to you, since there will still remain the tasks of putting them into the system, creating records, receiving, processing and cataloguing.

Donations

Donations are the most common source of free materials and should all be greeted in the same manner. It is good for public relations to accept donations gratefully on the basis that you will then decide what to do with them. Any restrictions on storage and use may restrict usefulness and have to be negotiated. They should all be formally acknowledged and donation labels put in items where appropriate – for example, if a book has been donated by its author. Figure 7.3 shows a sample letter of acknowledgement. Beware of any donors who basically want you to pay. Beware also of items which arrive unordered and appear to be free, but for which an invoice appears some days later. You are not obliged to accept or pay for such materials. It is important that donations fit your collection. They should only be put into stock on this basis.

If the author of an important new work is in your institution, it is perfectly acceptable to approach them for a 'free' copy, although this will not always work. Requesting the author's signature, and making sure to send a personal letter of acknowledgement, will help with future donations, as will occasional displays of works by 'local' authors. If you want to get more donations you can

Taylor Institution Library
Oxford University Library Services

From the Librarian
elizabeth.chapman@taylib.ox.ac.uk

Taylor Institution Library
University of Oxford
St Giles', Oxford OX1 3NA
Tel: 01865 278160 / 278154
Fax: 01865 278165

Professor A. Language-Specialist
St Something's College
OXFORD OX1 1XX

18 January 2004

Dear Professor Language-Specialist,

I am writing to thank you very much indeed for the copy of your book *A complete history of foreign literature* which you were kind enough to present to the Library a little while ago.

We are delighted to have been given such a useful and interesting book, which we would otherwise have had to purchase out of our ever-shrinking acquisitions budget, and I know that it will be most appreciated by many of our readers.

You might like to know that all such donations are given a special bookplate with the donor's name on it and donors also receive an honourable mention in the Library's Annual Report.

Once again, thank you very much for thinking of this Library.

Yours sincerely,

Ms E.A. Chapman
Librarian

Figure 7.3   Sample letter of acknowledgement for a donation

register your collection or library on *amazon.com* to receive items.

Donations of runs of journals are more difficult to deal with. The cheapest solution is simply to send them elsewhere. If they fill a gap on your shelves, well and good, but the cost of checking should not exceed purchase costs, and nor should you be filling up the shelves with things to which you have an electronic subscription.

Exchanges

An exchange agreement exists when one institution agrees to send out its publications regularly to another institution, which will send something roughly equivalent in return. As an example, exchanges of academic working papers have been common, but more and more of this material is becoming available on the web. Exchanges are a good way of getting hold of the publications of institutions like yours in other countries, and official publications not readily available through normal channels. Exchanges are time-consuming to set up and to administer. If your exchange partner is effectively sending you something free, it is difficult to complain when items do not turn up on a regular basis. Just like donations they are not free because of the processing costs involved. On top of this you may well have to pay for material which you are sending out on exchange. A good rule of thumb as to whether to set up or continue an exchange is to consider whether you would be prepared to buy the materials you are receiving on exchange, whether they are actually available for purchase, and whether in monetary terms what you get represents a fair exchange.

A time to refrain from ordering

Faced with a list of unobtainable items, interlibrary loan is one way you can at least review a title before deciding whether to pursue it further. This may be enough to satisfy the original requester. Alternatively, you may be able to direct users to collections with more of the materials they want, using some of the sources mentioned in Chapter 4. There will always remain some titles you will be unable to purchase. These include: publications which are 'classified' and therefore not available to the general public, materials which are intended for qualified users only such as psychological tests, and material which is announced but which for whatever reason never sees the light of day. Titles which are banned, however, are sometimes possible to get hold of, possibly via a foreign dealer, particularly if the ban is imposed after publication. The growth of electronic publications means that while you may not be able to actually own a particular item, you may be able to provide access to it.

8

When the orders arrive

The mail

Acquisitions departments receive huge amounts of mail every day. Sifting through this, you will be able to direct a good deal of it towards other interested parties, since much of it will be advertisements for future publications, or even fit for the circular file. What you should deal with expeditiously are fulfilled orders coming in. The hard work of checking and ordering will be wasted unless parcels are attended to promptly. You cannot complain about slow delivery unless you act quickly when deliveries do appear.

Acquisitions work seldom runs evenly. Work rarely arrives in an even flow, but has a tendency to come in large amounts all at once. One way to attempt to control the flow is to arrange with your major suppliers to deliver on a regular basis – say, once a week. However, suppliers suffer from the same uneven flow, and they will probably consolidate your orders until they have enough material to warrant sending out a parcel. If a carrier is used for transport they too may consolidate deliveries.

Checking in orders

Always open parcels carefully, since some will be more sensibly packaged than others. Do not use untrained staff to open parcels. They will not be on the lookout for concealed invoices or reports, which can easily get lost. Some invoices are folded up and sealed in plastic on the front of parcels to form the address label. These are about as easy to open without damage as the plastic-wrapped cheese from the supermarket. In the case of electronic materials, some of these will constitute a contract which you agree to, simply by opening the parcel. Pre-paid orders, on the other hand, may lack paperwork altogether. A quick cut with a sharp knife through the outer wrappings of a parcel can go through paper covers and invoices in one fell swoop. Scissors are recommended for everyone's safety.

Once the parcel is unpacked, check off the items against the invoice or delivery note to ensure that the following are what you expect:

- author and title
- edition
- format
- number of copies/volumes
- condition (appearance, damage in transit)
- servicing
- price
- discount.

If the check is satisfactory, the next action is to call up the original records on your order system. The ISBN or order number is often the quickest key to get back to the order. Review again that what you expected has arrived and change the status of the record from 'on order' to 'arrived', using whatever terminology is provided on your system. Making an item 'arrive' tells your users that it is available. Acquisitions also needs to know how much it has cost so that budgets and financial records are kept up to date. Information from the invoice will have to be put on the system so that committed and balance figures can be recalculated. Final invoice totals seldom match the figures you commit at order stage. Prices of materials and their delivery go up and discounts may go down. This is often the point at which a barcode number is added to the item and its record. Figure 8.1 shows an order system receiving screen.

Invoices

Make certain that invoices have been charged to the correct fund or section on the order system. Some institutions simply pay all materials purchases on a single departmental code, and keep the division of the in-house funds and of their accounting as an internal procedure. However, if you run an automated order system, you should use it to its fullest capacity, and dealing with separate funds can be happily assigned to computers. Figure 8.2 shows an invoice screen from an automated system with invoice details.

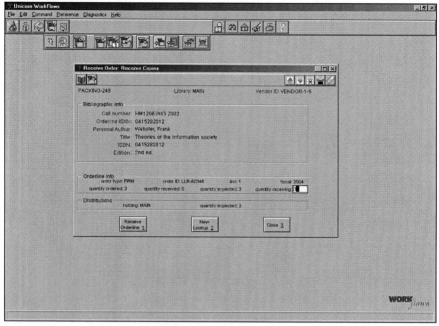

Figure 8.1   Order system receiving screen

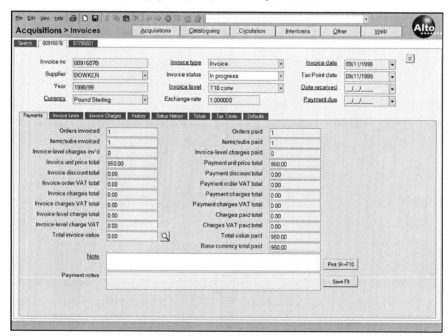

Figure 8.2   Existing invoice record showing invoice details

To clear and approve an invoice for payment usually includes the following steps:

- dating the invoice with the date the delivery arrived
- checking the items on the invoice against the original order
- sorting out any immediate problems
- checking that order numbers appear by the correct items on the invoice
- checking that fund accounts are allocated correctly
- checking prices and discounts
- checking totals are correct
- adding a mark of approval and recognized name to clear payment.

In some financial systems further documentation will be needed to request payment, but more frequently action on the actual invoice is sufficient. Acquisitions should keep a copy of all invoices to file. Paper invoices are best filed by date in reverse order (most recent at the front of the file), so that if there is a query later on you can tell the supplier the date they issued the invoice. Your date of receipt will not be known to them. Major suppliers warrant their own file, with occasional suppliers filed alphabetically. Copying details of invoices into ledgers, whether they are automated or not, is a waste of time and prone to error. The finance office will anyway keep a purchase ledger. If your finance system does not produce monthly figures for you on money spent, this is the point at which a running total can be kept, by fund if necessary.

Paperless invoicing

EDI, as mentioned in Chapter 6, allows for electronic paperless ordering and invoicing, fed directly into and out of your automated system. However, you must be sure that there is communication between acquisitions and finance, preferably electronically, so that invoices are actually paid. The auditors will still want to be sure that payment is approved, as described in Chapter 9.

Delivery problems

If you have a reliable supplier who knows clearly what your requirements are, you should not have too many problems at the check-in stage. But every once in a while there will be errors and you should have an established routine for handling each type. Some of the errors may have been caused by acquisitions, and some may be unavoidable. A list of the most common problems associated with each stage of the check-in procedure follows. In each case you should check further as indicated before rejecting material altogether:

1   The item is not the title ordered:
    Has the title changed between announcement and publication?
    Was the order correct?

2   The edition was not the one ordered:
    Is this item simply a paperback edition of a previous hardback?
    Was the order correct?

3   The format is wrong:
    Can you accept the wrong format, and if not can you face the consequent delay?
    Is there actually another format available?
    Was the order correct?

4   The number of copies is incorrect:
    Does the invoice say 'n' copies to follow?
    Can you accept the wrong number of copies, or do you need to re-order or get credit?
    Was the order correct?

5   The number of volumes (or the volume number) is incorrect:
    Does the invoice say volume 'n' to follow?
    Does one item contain all the volumes required?
    Was the order correct?

6   The material is in poor condition:
    If it is a book, flick through to check whether a gathering is missing, pages are missing, or pages are blank or printed upside down
    If it is second-hand you might expect some wear
    Is the damage sufficient to warrant return?

7   The price is incorrect:
    An increase in price between ordering and receipt is very common (see Chapter 9)
    An outrageous difference should be checked with the supplier/publisher
    Is there a previously unexpected handling charge?
    Is the price incorrectly transcribed, e.g. £1190 instead of £11.90?

8   The discount is incorrect:
    Has your consortium discount been omitted?
    Is this from a non-commercial supplier?

9   The servicing is incorrect:
    Is it acceptable as it is?
    Can it be rectified in-house?

10   The item received is not on order:
    Is this an urgent order which you ordered by e-mail/fax/telephone?
    Is this an outstanding order which you have already claimed and received?
    Have you recently cancelled this order?
    Is this a response to a simple request for information?
    Is the whole parcel for another department/institution?
    Does this order repeat one already received?
    Is this item a donation?
    Is this an unsolicited order from someone who hopes you will pay for it?

11   There is no invoice:
    Is the invoice still somewhere in or on the packaging?
    Is the invoice inside the material?
    Have you already paid a pro-forma invoice?
    Did you order by credit card?
    Has the order been sent direct by the publisher although you ordered from usual supplier?
    Is this an inspection copy/donation/exchange?

12   There is an invoice but no materials to match:
    Is it a pro-forma invoice?
    Is the invoice intended for another department/institution?
    Is it actually an order for something produced by your institution?
    Is it a statement/credit note?

13   The item you expect has not arrived (see section on Claims below).

If after considering all the possibilities you cannot accept the items in question, you should return them. Do not forget to alter your order records if you have already changed their status, and ask your supplier for the correct item and for credit if necessary. If only part of the order has arrived, be careful to ensure that your records are updated accordingly.

Returns and credit

Part of your agreement with any supplier should be a policy on how to handle returns. Suppliers will accept that they sometimes make mistakes and you must accept that acquisitions sometimes makes mistakes too. How willing the supplier will be to take back your mistakes will vary, and will probably depend amongst other things on how good a customer you are in financial terms. However, some items will be marked 'non-returnable' on the invoice. You can rightly claim postage costs on the supplier's mistakes but not on yours. It may be possible to return books via the next delivery, but you need to contact the supplier so that the carrier is alerted to collect as well as to deliver next time they call.

There are several ways of handling credit after returns or other problems. Here are some possibilities, starting with the most practical solutions and going on to the least efficient ones:

1   Pay the whole invoice and request credit for the disputed items.
2   Issue a self-credit as provided for by the supplier.
3   Delete the offending item from the invoice and pay the rest (unlikely to be acceptable to accountants at either end).
4   Request an amended invoice (slow).
5   Return the item and the invoice if it is a single-item invoice (be prepared to see the original invoice turn up on statements for the next few years).

Whichever method you choose, you must contact the supplier first and keep very careful records of your actions. The supplier will want to know at least your account number, the author and title of the item, the order number, the invoice number and the invoice date. Credit notes are passed to finance to deal with just like invoices, and indeed they often look much like invoices, so need to be checked carefully. A copy should be filed on your acquisitions system. Do not forget to credit the correct fund on your order system.

Unless your system allows for an electronic interchange, standard letters can be used for returns; see Figure 8.3 for an example. Acquisitions staff time is also money and a mistaken second copy may not radically alter the balance of your stock. The return of material which has already been serviced by the supplier is unlikely to be possible. Try to establish a price below which it is not worth

Taylor Institution Library
Oxford University Library Services

From the Librarian
elizabeth.chapman@taylib.ox.ac.uk

Taylor Institution Library
University of Oxford
St Giles', Oxford OX1 3NA
Tel: 01865 278160 / 278154
Fax: 01865 278165

A.N.Y. Bookseller plc
999 High Street
OXFORD OX1 XXX

18 January 2004

Dear A.N.Y. Bookseller,

Account number: ....

Order number:..

Order date: ...... / ...... / ......

We are returning the enclosed item to you for the following reason:

1. wrong title
2. wrong edition
3. duplicate
4. incorrect no. of copies sent
5. not our order
6. defective copy

7. ....

Please kindly do the following:

1. send credit
2. replace with a perfect copy
3. re-order the following title instead:

4. ....

Thank you very much.

Yours sincerely,

Ms E.A. Chapman
Librarian

Figure 8.3 Sample letter to suppliers explaining returns

returning an unwanted item with all the staff time that implies, and try to find a good home for it.

Cancellations

If you decide that something you have ordered is no longer required, you can cancel the order. Cancellations, like returns, should be agreed with your supplier, as should a procedure for handling them. You may not be able to cancel orders which have already been despatched, either from the publisher or from the supplier. Occasionally they may accept such a cancellation in order to promote good relations, but you should not let it happen too frequently. The cancellation of standing orders is a formal procedure and should be put in writing to your supplier.

Outstanding orders can be cancelled automatically after an agreed length of time. The supplier can inform you of what is being cancelled and give you the option of re-ordering (surprisingly this sometimes works when the item previously seemed to be unobtainable). The length of time at which you set automatic cancellations should be discussed with your supplier, since they will have broader experience of how long certain types of material take to arrive. Do not forget to take action to alter records on your order system and to inform anyone requesting the material that the order has been cancelled. Cancellation frees up committed funds for other purchases.

Reports

If the material which you have ordered does not appear, you should be given a report by your supplier. The usual format for a report is: order number, author, title, report code and date. Reports do not always mean that the order will not be supplied. Reports can arrive electronically; they sometimes come by post separately or in parcels with other orders. You can pick up your own reports if you have a query on a specific order and Figure 8.4 shows such an enquiry being made of a supplier's system. If reports reach your order system directly, that is excellent, but e-mail reports mean a good deal of work to collate the information and transfer it to the order records. You can arrange whichever route you would prefer, but do not expect single reports, for these like orders are generally consolidated for economy of effort. Do not ignore them, but take action to alter order records and inform those requesting the material.

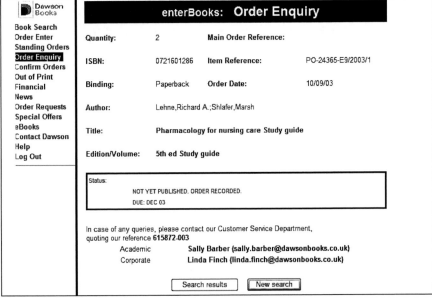

Figure 8.4   Checking for a supplier's report on an order

Here is a list of some of the most common report codes you might encounter:

AUTOCANC   automatic cancellation date reached

BDG   binding

CT   cannot trace as available

NAA   not available on approval

NE   new edition in preparation

NK   not known by publisher

NR   no sales rights in this country

NRFP   no reply from publisher

NYP   not yet published

OP   out of print

OS   out of stock

PUBABAND   publication abandoned

RP   reprinting

RP/ND   reprinting – no date set

TOS   temporarily out of stock

Claims

If you do not receive either the items you have ordered or a report, you should send a claim or chaser to the supplier. You will be able to work out from your average arrival time for orders when a claim should go out. Allow up to 90 days in which to receive an order – less for a report. Of course most orders will arrive more quickly than that, but an efficient supplier will also be claiming on your behalf in the meantime.

Automated order systems will enthusiastically generate claims according to the parameters of time and supplier that you set up. The work of claiming on manual order files is speeded up considerably if you keep copies of the original order which can simply be marked 'claim' and sent to the supplier. Claims should be clearly marked as such, wherever they come from, or they may be mistaken for new orders. While individual claims can be sent on standard letters, automated systems allow for customized wording to suit all claiming occasions.

Claims for pre-paid orders should not wait 90 days. Perhaps 40 days would be enough in this instance, particularly if you find out that the money you have sent has been banked. Chasing pre-paid orders should be relentless until you are sure something is happening. Try all the methods of communication available to you. If the item is not yet published it obviously will not appear for a while, but the publisher or supplier should keep you informed. Pre-paid orders from small non-commercial publishers may be delayed simply because there are too few staff to deal with them quickly. Send paper claims by first-class mail, or airmail if they are going abroad. Acquisitions needs a record of what has been claimed and when. Figure 8.5 shows a system claims window.

Accessions

Although accessions is a part of the procedure of buying materials, and is sometimes confused with the whole of acquisitions, it is only a small but fairly important procedure which happens at the moment when materials are accepted into stock by acquisitions. Once acquisitions has covered all the check-in procedures, items can be passed on to other staff for cataloguing or processing. At this point you should be collecting statistics on how many items have been bought and how many were on exchange or 'free'. Nothing should move from acquisitions until it belongs to the institution – that is, it has either been paid for or definitely does not have to be paid for. If you allow anything to

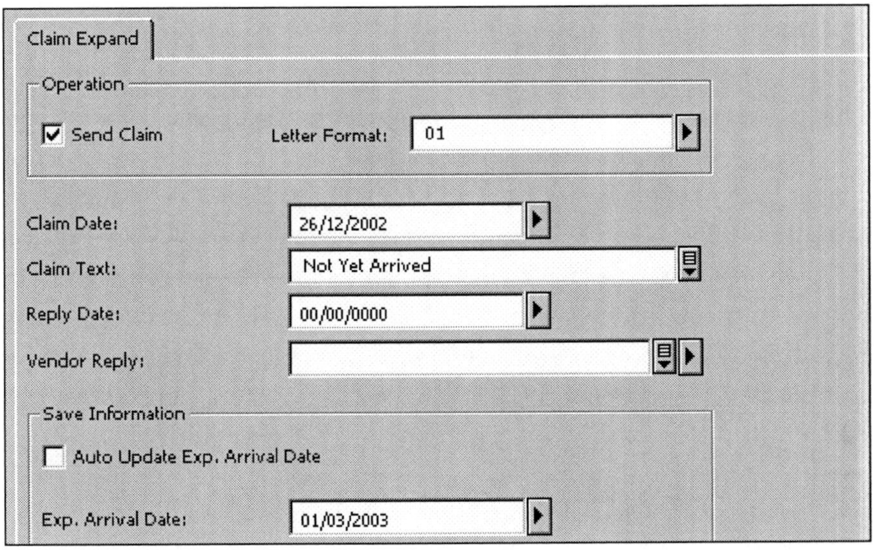

Figure 8.5 System claims window

move on before you have paid for it, you are almost bound to face problems later on when invoices are checked.

Of course an urgent order can be rushed through, but not without acquisitions keeping track of all the usual details by making a careful record. Liaison with cataloguing, which may well be part of the same staffing area, is crucial both in the day-to-day operation of acquisitions and in the rush order situation. Tagging an item 'urgent' without previously setting up a procedure to deal with this may not work well. Information on whether the item has some special attribute, such as reserved, new edition, added copy, continuation, can be helpful in speeding the catalogue record. In the best-case scenario, cataloguing copy already exists at least in skeleton form on the database, as it was found at the pre-order stage, so all that is needed is an enhancement of the record. If catalogue records are sent by your supplier with orders, this too will speed the process. Some few items may have by-passed the pre-order check, and searching for a catalogue record will have to start from scratch.

It used to be the case that all new items were entered in an accessions register with a running number being allocated. However, so long as an item is to be catalogued in some way, and copy invoices which are filed hold details of individual titles, the practice of accession numbering is not strictly necessary. Automated systems will anyway allocate control numbers for each item.

Announcing the new arrivals

As new materials move into stock they should be announced to users. There are various ways of doing this, ranging from specialized lists printed or posted on websites or sent to interested users, through displays of new material, to announcements in the library's newsletter or via e-mail. After all the hard work and expense of acquisitions, it makes sense to announce what has arrived, and also to market it to some extent. Users are not yet used to looking for metadata on new databases in the catalogue, and in all likelihood they will need some introduction or training to use such services, so non-book announcements in particular should be prominent. Metadata in this context is simply data about data which can be read by computers – a kind of electronic cataloguing of electronic materials. Checking the lists of new materials announced in other specialized collections may actually be helpful if you are building up a particular area.

Statistics

All the work involved in buying materials needs to be recorded. The budget holders, whether private or public, will want to know how the money has been spent. Operational statistics in terms of items bought are not only a requirement for acquisitions, but are useful for future planning of budgets and workflow. Collecting and reviewing statistics on a monthly basis gives a good idea of how work is progressing and makes the burden of collecting statistics for the annual report that much lighter at the end of the year.

Operational statistics can be collected and displayed, using a simple spreadsheet program. They should include at least the following with both a monthly and running total:

- items bought
- items donated
- items received on exchange
- requests received/checked
- orders sent to suppliers.

Financial statistics are considered in Chapter 9.

9
Finance and budgets

Financial guidelines

An important part of acquisitions work concerns finance and budgets, and it is an area for which staff are seldom trained. Yet it can be very interesting work, not least because there is a measurable outcome. In acquisitions the financial areas are basically: budgeting, paying invoices and keeping records. In an era where regulation is growing, there will be institutional and national guidelines and policies for acquisitions to follow for financial probity. Procedures and policies have to be followed by acquisitions staff which allow for professional scrutiny from auditors. Even if you use a central accounts office to make payments, you will probably still keep your own in-house records as you will have different and more immediate information needs.

Budgets

Acquisitions work will be operating to a budget, and it is important to realize why you need one and how it is constructed. Budgets to some extent define the organization, and certainly define what it intends to achieve during the financial year. This framework gives the basis for planning expenditure. The budget is part of a system which should promote efficiency and effectiveness, and be able to provide information to show where individual departments have fallen short or exceeded expectations. Keeping a regular eye on the budget allows for variances during the year and for bidding for more money where necessary or possible. The budget outcome for any one year will be crucial in setting the budget for the following year. Not spending your acquisitions budget may give the impression that you do not need all the money you have been allocated. A budget is a form of centralized control, although for day-to-day operations certain sums of money will be allocated to acquisitions. In the final analysis the acquisitions budget will be weighed against those for staffing and other institutional needs.

There are various stages in setting a budget, and while acquisitions will not always be involved in setting the overall budget, an idea of how it is constructed is useful to provide a context for your work. Firstly the organization will be setting overall objectives both for the year ahead and probably for the longer, say, five-year term. Objectives can be reached by identifying strategies to reach those objectives, such as buying more electronic materials to support the work of the organization. Various options will be considered which will eventually lead to a strategic plan, which in turn needs an operations budget to support the agreed strategy. A good deal of notice will be taken of previous budget outcomes and during the year performance against estimates will be monitored, to check on variances and make corrections if necessary. Acquisitions needs to be ready with up-to-date information at any point in the year and with explanations of why one particular fund may seem to be overspending. You can use your own and your supplier's system to help you control expenditure. Figure 9.1 shows a supplier analysis of standing order expenditure.

Once the library or information service has been allocated a budget, there will be further work to split the budget into meaningful categories for expenditure. The acquisitions or materials budget can be divided in many different ways. Some services will be divided by subject area, according to previously agreed formulae, some will be divided by material type such as serials, books and electronic materials, while others will be divided by users such as adults, children and young adults. Some will need a hybrid budget, where some materials are paid for by acquisitions, and others are charged out to individual departments in the organization. Splitting by material type is becoming more and more questionable as new formats appear and to some extent overtake existing print formats. Budgets for serials have notoriously squeezed budgets for books over the last two decades and some balance needs to be maintained on behalf of users. Purchasing via a consortium may also affect your budget calculations. In some cases your institution may insist on using particular suppliers and/or e-procurement according to their set criteria. This can cause considerable problems to acquisitions staff because suppliers, who are used to supplying reams of paper, may not necessarily understand modern publishing, nor can they necessarily interface with library systems.

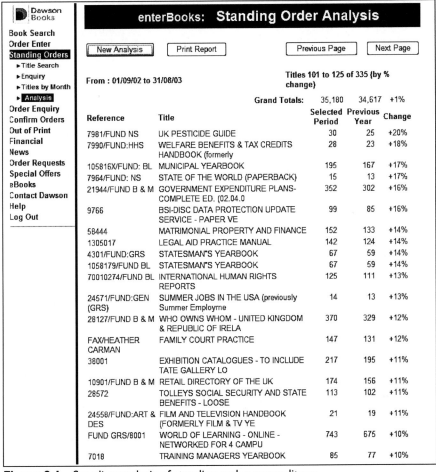

Figure 9.1   Supplier analysis of standing order expenditure

Criteria for determining allocations will need to include:

- the number of potential users
- the level of use – are multiple copies/multi-user licences needed?
- the breadth of existing stock and its potential obsolescence
- publishing output in relevant areas
- the price of materials
- previous expenditure
- institutional objectives.

No acquisitions department would ever describe its budget as being large enough, but one important factor is to keep some part of the budget – perhaps 10% – for contingencies such as unexpected but much-needed expenditure, or to bail out an individual fund which has overspent because of foreign currency fluctuations. Drawing up estimates for the year's expenditure is time-consuming but important work. With an automated accounts and/or acquisitions system you will be able to track progress during the year and make changes where necessary. The system can be set up, or you can set up a separate spreadsheet, to alert you automatically to notable variances. Estimates are not cast in stone, and equally publications do not appear with a nice regular flow during the year, but you should check carefully, at least on a monthly basis, what is happening.

Prices

Cynical acquisitions staff would say that any discount on published prices that you can get from your supplier is more than offset by the increase in price which occurs between the time you send off the order and the time when it arrives. In this respect the kinds of materials acquisitions purchases are different from other commodities with fixed prices. The publisher's setting of a price has to depend on such variables as the number of copies printed, the quality of production, the likely number of sales and the cost of marketing. Prices are often announced well ahead of publication, perhaps before a book has been written or a database compiled. In the case of books, a minimum price is usually set at the point where the author signs a contract. This point will often turn out to be more than a year before publication, despite the increase in production speed which the use of automation has achieved.

Author delays, production delays and increases in overhead costs can force the price upwards before publication. While it seems reasonable to say that you should not order something for which you do not know the price, if you know the item exists but cannot confirm the price you should still order it. The cost of getting price information should not exceed the benefit of actually getting it. A good relationship with your suppliers will allow you to get quotations before supply, or to put in an agreed guesstimate figure on your order which they will recognize. This will alert them to let you know if the eventual price goes above your agreed maximum. Usually acquisitions will have the freedom to purchase up to an agreed maximum, before needing to have an expensive order sanctioned elsewhere. If your users need an expensive item and your budget can afford it, you should buy it, even if you deplore the pricing.

Electronic materials are particularly affected by price uncertainties or fluctuations. Some of the factors affecting this are:

- electronic versions may only be available to print purchasers of the same product
- products may be bundled together
- there are different versions of the same product
- costs will vary according to the number of users or passwords allocated
- archive files may cost extra
- you may only be able to purchase via a consortium
- prices can vary between consortia
- different formats have different prices
- downloading and/or printing charges may be extra.

Foreign prices

Pricing the supply of materials from other countries is especially difficult. Currency exchange rate fluctuations can alter prices considerably, quite apart from the actions of publishers. Suppliers of foreign materials will usually convert prices at prevailing exchange rates and then add bank charges. Some will demand payment in a more stable currency such as US dollars, if their own currency is volatile. This can lead to double bank charges where your finance office charges to send foreign funds and then the receiving bank charges on receipt of the funds. Exchange rates and bank charges can play havoc with estimates. Discuss foreign pricing and payment with your suppliers and your finance office to get the best outcome for your budget.

Discount prices

Since the death of the Net Book Agreement in the UK, which allowed for an across-the-board discount, there has been further discounting of books, but this should be approached with caution. Consortium purchasing, mentioned in Chapter 5, also allows for discount prices. You may be able to make individual deals with your suppliers, but there are dwindling numbers of these and profit margins, particularly on books, are small. Some suppliers work on fixed discounts across the board, whereas others apply a sliding scale.

Price indexes

There are some surveys of publishers' prices which you may find useful when drawing up a budget. An index of prices is made by taking a certain year as a base. During the base year an average price for a group of materials – for example, fiction or sociology – is computed. In subsequent years the average cost of the same group is worked out and an index figure produced by calculating the percentage change (usually an increase). This index can be compared with the annual retail price index. In the case of the UK, USA and Germany, we can see price rises above inflation for books over the 1990s, and, in the 21st century, price rises for serials well above the rises for books. There are some signs that such increases are slowing for books, but publishing output is increasing. For serials, prices are continuing to cause serious concern.

Book price indexes for UK and US books (LISUb) are available from Loughborough University Library and Information Statistics Unit (LISU), as well as more general statistical reports (LISUa). Other bodies such as the Publishers' Association and SCONUL in the UK, and ARL in the USA, produce pricing and spending reports from time to time.

The financial year

The financial year, whenever it begins or ends, puts a good deal of artificially created pressure on acquisitions. Few financial years are the same as the calendar year, although some may coincide with the tax year. For UK local government the year runs from 1 April and for UK higher education from 1 August, while the academic year currently runs from September in schools and October in universities. Publishers of printed materials have two peak periods of publication in spring and autumn.

The budget for acquisitions may not be finally agreed until well into the new financial year, not least because there will be several departments competing for funds. At any rate materials seldom appear the moment they are ordered, so acquisitions will enter each financial year with a certain amount of money already committed. It might be possible, if your budget is severely cut, to start the year with little money to spend since so much is committed. In a time of budget cuts there will be times of the year when you simply cannot place orders as there will not be funds to pay invoices. Stockpiling orders is dangerous as new material can go rapidly out of print. On the other extreme there may be times, just before the financial year ends, when the institution you work for unexpectedly finds some money which needs spending very quickly. Be sure to have a shopping list readily available for this purpose, and a reputation for spending money both wisely and quickly. Your suppliers can usually cope with a glut of money.

To help you plan for any eventuality, including next year's budget, make sure you have to hand figures on:

- the budget – how much money is there to spend overall in the year?
- money committed – what amount of money is committed to orders not yet arrived (also known as encumbered figures)?
- money spent – how much money has actually been spent?
- the balance – how much money is left?

You should be able to obtain these figures from your automated order system, from your suppliers or from your finance office, but you may need a combination of all three, including some calculations of your own. It is best to consider these figures on a monthly basis, but probably more frequently near the end of the financial year. A simple spreadsheet can be used to help you see clearly how the budget is going. At the end of the financial year you must not forget to carry committed figures over to the next financial year as a charge on your new budget. Your suppliers need to be informed about possible payment delays. Finance officers believe that you really can stop ordering and receiving at the end of the financial year, and that all materials will have arrived before the end of the financial year, or if they have not arrived you will know exactly when they will, and exactly what they will cost, or you will cancel them. You may have to complete documentation calculating when your outstanding orders will arrive and how much they will cost, in order to sign off the end of the financial year. You will probably not have much time to spare on this particular work of fiction.

Invoices and payment

As explained in Chapter 5, acquisitions staff should have agreed with suppliers how, when and where invoices for materials supplied are to be presented. Whether these invoices are electronic or paper, it is worth considering in detail both sides of the bargain. You want the most useful invoices you can get and the supplier wants prompt payment. You will want to consider the following elements as more or less crucial for your invoices:

- invoice number and date
- customer name and account number
- address/bank details for payment
- address for queries including: telephone, fax, e-mail
- acquisitions order number against each item supplied
- fund to be charged if relevant
- information on items supplied including: author, title, number of copies, number of volumes
- status information such as standing order
- reports on non-supply (see Chapter 8)
- financial information including: publisher's list price, discount %, carriage, tax, total
- terms of payment, e.g. payment required in 30 days
- currency requirements
- how many copies you need (paper invoices) – e.g. one for passing for payment, one for filing
- date and method of dispatch by supplier.

Receipt of material is described in Chapter 8, but it must be mentioned here that for the sake of efficiency both the supplier and your finance department should know what is expected in the way of invoicing. Make an effort to visit and maintain links with the person who will handle your payments. This will greatly help to smooth any future concerns such as an urgent payment. If you can visit each other's offices, you can get a feel for their work and priorities and they can do more to understand yours. By doing this you will understand that there is no point in writing a message to a supplier on a paper invoice passed for payment, as the invoice itself will simply be filed, and funds will be passed to a bank electronically. Remember too that the finance office are just as busy as acquisitions, and just as prone to peaks and troughs, and cannot always pay invoices at the moment you want them to, so you may well get statements and reminders which you do not expect.

Do not overload the finance staff with payments in huge batches, but try to keep an even flow by clearing invoices regularly at least once a week. The finance office probably do the same, but make sure to find out what the final cut-off date will be for any month, and the cut-off date for foreign currency payments, which may be different. Discuss whether they can easily cope with foreign payments, how they will charge you, and discuss any such decisions with your supplier. Keep a wary eye open to check that agreed policies are indeed implemented. The finance office will periodically provide you with information on how your accounts are being spent. Make sure you know what these figures mean from the way they are set out, and if you do not understand them, ask for help. You should check these reports for glaring discrepancies such as payments allocated to you from some other department, or an unexpectedly high payment which you do not remember.

Automation has greatly altered the work of acquisitions staff, at the same time as accounts departments are increasingly automated. Getting these two areas to interface their respective computer systems has so far been slow but is improving. Lack of interface between systems results in a need to re-key, send or print further information to supplement what the finance office can give you. Automated library systems are becoming more sophisticated in the acquisitions area, and will be able to include such information as: price, foreign price, currency conversion, fund accounts, charge-out details, department codes, checks on budgets, invoice details. Again, interfaces between library management systems and supplier systems have been slow to evolve but are improving. The era of paperless accounting is not yet quite here, although electronic signature helps. As long as you have to deal with smaller niche publishers it will be some time before you can achieve paperless accounting. Many systems can generate reports for you, as well as standard letters, and can link with the spreadsheets you may need to set up for individual funds. Your system should also be able to provide you with the financial history of any individual order. Figure 9.2 shows a review of funds on an automated order system.

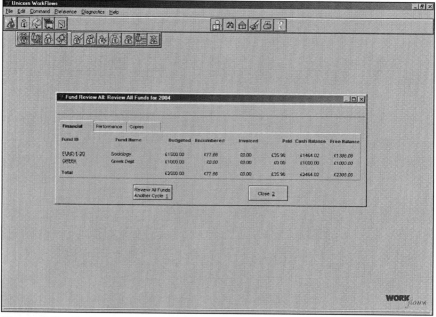

Figure 9.2   Order system review of funds

Pro-forma invoices and pre-payment

Pro-forma invoices are sent to acquisitions when you have to pay before the order can be supplied. They are disliked both by acquisitions and by accounts, but you will need to have a method of requesting such payment. This will usually involve some bureaucratic form-filling to request payment. These forms and other requests for payment are known in accounting parlance as vouchers. Pre-payment may be the only way you can get certain materials and sometimes they have the advantage of avoiding delivery costs, enhancing discount or indeed using up money quickly before the end of the financial year. Very large pre-payments should be checked carefully with colleagues or with reputable suppliers if you are in any doubt about the recipient of your money.

After pre-payment has been sent, your order system must be capable of checking periodically that the item has arrived. It must also issue chasers if the item has not arrived. Items which are pre-paid sometimes arrive with what looks like an invoice masquerading as a receipt. Look carefully for the note saying that it has already been paid, and file as you would any other paid invoice. If the item fails to arrive, ask for credit.

Credit and purchase cards

With the increasing number of orders being placed electronically on the internet, a credit card has become a useful attribute in acquisitions. Institutions are granting this possibility to purchasing departments under certain controls. In fact some acquisitions departments are not using true credit cards but procurement cards with definite budgetary limits. The advantages of such cards for acquisitions include:

- speed – they can be used for immediate and urgent orders from a range of suppliers
- good for out-of-print as well as new material, and particularly good for foreign suppliers
- reduction of paperwork – no orders or individual invoices change hands
- individual cheques do not have to be written
- no bank charges/currency conversion charges
- good foreign currency exchange rates can be enjoyed
- they can eliminate the need for petty cash.

The disadvantages include:

- purchase order details still need to be keyed into the order system
- payment will have to be allocated to the relevant fund
- statements do not include details of individual titles
- spending limits may be low
- suppliers have to pay a 1–2% credit-card company fee
- complex requirements for reconciling with finance office
- loss of the discount enjoyed with usual suppliers
- possible fraudulent use of card.

If you decide that a credit or purchasing card would be useful for acquisitions you will need to consider the points above, and also decide on the level of security you will need. Usually only one person can be the designated cardholder and signatory – a responsibility that cannot be delegated. They will have to ensure that the card is held securely in a safe place. A spending limit on the card will be agreed with the finance office, and possibly a limit to the kinds of materials that can be purchased. For example, it might be used for new or second-hand materials but not for ongoing subscriptions. Current security advice, when giving credit card details over the internet, is to split the details between at least two messages. Auditing procedures for purchases on a credit card will also need to be agreed, and seem so far to be carried out rather more frequently than ordinary auditing. This may be because we know that using a credit card can encourage the most careful shopper to overspend. Your acquisitions system can provide an electronic purchase log which may be acceptable to the auditors.

Statements

Statements come to acquisitions from suppliers to inform you which invoices have been paid and which remain unpaid. This section does not apply to credit card statements, which are in effect invoices. Statements usually appear regularly, either on a monthly or on a quarterly basis, but from smaller suppliers may only appear near the end of their financial year, when they are trying to chase outstanding payments. Some suppliers send out statements almost immediately after sending out invoices. Some acquisitions departments only pay when they receive statements, but this is not good practice as statements contain much less detail than invoices, and it is therefore difficult to know what you are paying for. At any rate your finance office will probably refuse to pay on a statement. Some statements have the word 'statement' so well concealed that you can be fooled into paying twice.

Of course, if you do not pay invoices when they are due, and you ignore statements, you may well receive a suitably embellished letter from a solicitor or from a credit chasing agency. Do not ignore these but investigate at once, even if you think you have already paid or they are not really for your department. You may be able to persuade your finance department to check statements, but if not you really should check them. It will be a matter of how much time you have. At least give them a cursory glance and check out any items which are really old or really big. If you find that there are items which you have not paid for, ask the supplier for a copy invoice, and pass this to finance with a clear indication that it is 'not previously paid'. In normal circumstances, finance offices will not pay on copy invoices. As Figures 9.3 and 9.4 show, you can find out more about invoices received and paid from your order system or your suppliers' systems.

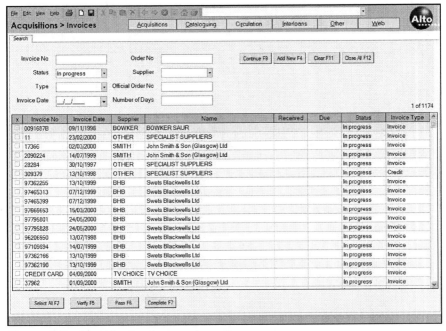

Figure 9.3   Checking invoices on the order system

Credit notes

The obtaining and issue of credit is dealt with in Chapter 8. If you have a credit note to deal with, this is passed to finance in the same way as an invoice, but the finance office may request you to draw it to their attention by marking it in a particular way. This is because credit notes tend to look much like invoices.

Financial records and auditing

Acquisitions staff are seldom trained accountants, but you will need to deal with accountants and follow professionally recognized ways of keeping records. It is important to keep good financial records anyway, not just because they may be audited, but so that you can keep track of what is happening to your budget. There are three possible levels of independent audit which you may come across. The first and most frequent will be the internal audit, run by professionals from your finance office. The next level is the external auditor employed from outside the institution, to provide an impartial view. The third level is one you hope never to meet, where those who fund your institution call

Dawson Books	enterBooks: **Invoices On-line**			
Book Search				
Order Enter	**Results**		Next Page	New Search
Standing Orders				
Order Enquiry	1 to 25 of 288	Result Pages: 1 2 3 4 5 6 7 8 9 10 11 12		
Confirm Orders	**Document No.**	**Document Date**	**Document Type**	**Document Value**
Out of Print				
Financial	X743566	26 September 2003	Invoice	92.25
►Account Details				
►Invoices Online	X743570	26 September 2003	Invoice	20.74
News				
Order Requests	X743571	26 September 2003	Invoice	24.69
Special Offers				
eBooks	X741837	25 September 2003	Invoice	165.94
Contact Dawson				
Help	X742263	25 September 2003	Invoice	81.96
Log Out				
	X742264	25 September 2003	Invoice	174.41
	X742265	25 September 2003	Invoice	164.43
	X742266	25 September 2003	Invoice	190.76
	X742267	25 September 2003	Invoice	15.80
	X742402	25 September 2003	Invoice	128.55
	X742403	25 September 2003	Invoice	122.56
	X742404	25 September 2003	Invoice	136.48
	X740988	24 September 2003	Invoice	20.34
	X740989	24 September 2003	Invoice	224.84
	X740990	24 September 2003	Invoice	88.47

Figure 9.4 Checking invoices on a supplier system

in auditors because there are suspected financial problems.

The reasons why audits are held are to verify any financial records kept, and to check that financial operations are taking place in an agreed framework and according to the financial regulations which are in place. For acquisitions this means checking that orders have been properly authorized, received and paid, and that different people have checked and sanctioned these procedures. This is known as 'separation of duties' and is insisted upon in financial regulations to avoid fraud. For a small acquisitions section it may be difficult to find enough staff to separate duties in the preferred way and special arrangements will have to be made. While the advent of an auditor may seem threatening, it should not be viewed in this way. If things are working well financially you should not be worried, but be grateful for the extra pair of eyes advising you on procedures.

Accountants and auditors who spend whole weeks looking at very different departments from yours may well need some time to talk about what makes acquisitions tick. You will need to explain the vagaries of pricing, the delays in delivery and processing, and the fact that the material you purchased last year may well be out on loan now, or may be entirely electronic so not immediately tangible or visible. Auditors will find it difficult, for example, to understand that your committed figures (orders out) will not ultimately match expenditure figures (orders in), owing to such vagaries, mentioned earlier, as price increases or non-receipt. Internal auditors have tended to follow more than a financial checking route, and now look at all business processes to ensure good practice as well as financial probity. As an example of this, the auditor will probably want to know that you check the performance of your suppliers as described in Chapter 5.

Apart from looking at general acquisitions processes, auditors will also want to follow random audit trails, following an order through all its stages of request, order, committed funds, arrival, payment and processing. They will want to actually see the material and that it is suitably looked after. As already mentioned, they will want to check that you operate an agreed separation of duties, so that different people are placing orders, receiving and checking materials, sanctioning payment, sending off for payment and checking accounts statements or computer print-outs. They will want to be assured that all material received in one financial year is paid for during that year – a feat particularly difficult to achieve with foreign payments. They will want to know that you keep records for the agreed length of time, and that even tiny orders for postage stamps are correctly recorded. Petty cash records and receipts will also be checked. Your automated system and/or supplier system can be of some use in auditing and some systems provide audit trails, as Figure 9.5 shows. Auditors are usually keen on stocktaking, being unaware that this practice usually raises more queries than it solves. A sample stocktake may pacify them.

Following recent high profile corporate scandals, auditors are being extra scrupulous and careful in their reports. They work towards being able to issue a report in accordance with agreed standards. As well as examining evidence relevant to acquisitions sections on a test basis, they will have the wider institutional role of ensuring that estimates and final outcomes, as expressed in end of year statements, are free from mis-statement, whether caused by fraud, irregularity or error.

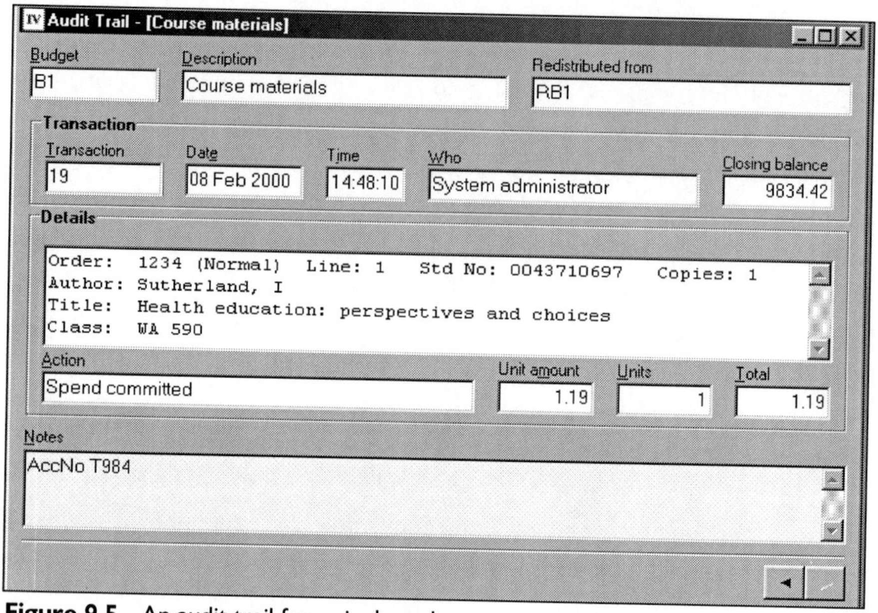

Figure 9.5 An audit trail for a single order

Being audited is much like failing your driving test. Even if you are generally competent to drive, the examiner may find a few things wrong, which although they are not crucial in themselves, add up to a potential danger. The auditor will provide you with a written report including recommendations for action, to which you will be able to respond. You should view this as helpful advice and by no means as threatening. You should also take the recommended action unless it is totally impractical. You can learn much from a good auditor and the report can provide backing when you are making a case for more time or staff to achieve the improved financial operation that the auditor suggests.

10
The way ahead

The work of acquisitions staff is constantly changing. On the one hand, these alterations in our operations have been forced on us by developments in the world of publishing, and, on the other, we have changed our procedures considerably in the light of automation, the internet and integrated library systems. What is certain is that further changes are in store and that this book can only whet your appetite for those.

The internet, with all the hype that surrounds it, has forced change on us, but has also provided us with some excellent answers to previous problems. What we need to do now is take the best of the internet and marry it with the best our suppliers can offer. Suppliers have been facing tough times, while continuing to enhance their services. Some of the smaller suppliers have been taken over or disappeared entirely. The amount of acquisitions work that is oursourced is small but growing. Our systems are now much more sophisticated, but we have to be careful not to continue to be involved in unnecessary detail or duplication of effort. We need our library systems to communicate electronically with our supplier systems, and we need our suppliers' systems to communicate properly with our finance systems. Only when that happens can we avoid re-keying information over and over again.

It seems that the announcement of the death of the book is premature – browsing bookshelves is still popular – but we must make use of the fact that we have some idea what is coming next. If we do not provide what our users want, or what we know they will want, we risk being overtaken by internet services which will cover the range of items we currently buy and go straight to the user, bypassing our service. So we have to make an effort to keep in touch with what is happening, and knowing about the world of publishing is a real responsibility for acquisitions. In the realm of distance or open learning, students will not necessarily visit our service, but will expect us to provide the materials that they want, wherever they want them.

E-books, even with their current drawbacks of expensive equipment and lack of industry standards, are still evolving in an uncertain market. For students and for professionals who need up-to-date information, there looks to be a market for e-books. However, initial offerings have not always done well, and some aggregators of e-books have disappeared, while publishers who were wary of aggregators are now taking up the challenge on their own behalf. The market seems to place more emphasis on individual titles than in its first phase, but it is growing. Travelling light will become more of a possibility. However, we cannot at the moment expect such things to last any better than older books, since digital preservation is now the equivalent of sticky tape on leather bindings. At the other end of a print book's life, the idea of an out-of-print book is becoming uncommon as we access secondhand dealers on the internet, and make use of internet auctions and the burgeoning print-on-demand services.

Quite apart from e-books, we now have so many format possibilities to consider – from print, print and electronic, online pay per use, database subscription and internet subscription, open archives to internet pay per use. The internet offers us many advantages, including searching across text and texts, and making links, even if some of these appear fugitive. On the internet you can order a book, read or write reviews on it, chat with other readers and even meet the author. However, none of this is free, even though it may seem like that. Although it is true at least in the area of second-hand book buying that searching across the internet can drive down prices. The computing infrastructure we need for acquisitions is increasing in capacity all the time, and searching on the internet is time-consuming too. We do not know how the internet will develop, but evidence shows that after the purchase of travel, the purchase of books is one of the highest earners on the internet, yet it has taken a while for it to be directed towards library and information services. We were not considered to be a big enough slice of the market. That perception has been tempered by the dawning realization that the library and information market is relatively low risk, and publishing has stable growth with an ability to charge pretty much what it wants, although there are growing signs of rebellion here.

There is some concern that if institutional budgets dwindle or stagnate, affected either by serials price increases or by factors outside our services, we shall all be buying the same materials, or at least access to them. The work of acquisitions includes seeking out the more fugitive materials, and making sure that they are accessible. The internet may be a good way to find information and for some publishers to make money, but we must not forget that acquisitions is in the business of providing a service. We shall have to use all the avenues open to us to find and acquire the materials that our users need. We have to keep all channels of communication open and be open to change ourselves. Time and convenience are crucial to our users, along with ease of use.

Keeping up with developments

It is the responsibility, then, of acquisitions to keep up to date on what is happening and make changes in our work. You can do this by reading relevant journals, searching the internet, and attending meetings and conferences. *AcqWeb* is one very good way of entering the world of acquisitions via the internet, but it may seem rather daunting at first. It is an excellent guide to resources for pre-order searching for all sorts of material both in and out of print, information on and from publishers, and information on suppliers. Relevant associations and organizations are listed, and selected publications on library science in general, and acquisitions in particular, are included. If you find something useful on *AcqWeb*, or indeed on the somewhat more general but genuinely international *BUBL*, you should bookmark the useful addresses. Both of these services will direct you to e-mail lists where you can join in discussions on current acquisitions topics or help out a colleague elsewhere. Reading journals and books is useful, and some of the more important ones for acquisitions are included in the further reading for this chapter. Attending meetings, book fairs and exhibitions can be very instructive. In the UK the National Acquisitions Group holds meetings, training courses and an annual conference, and publishes a newsletter and a journal. In the USA the Charleston Annual Acquisitions Conference has spawned more than one journal which may be of use. Acquisitions usually features as part of the larger professional association meetings, such as ALA (American Library Association), too.

All this may seem like a diversion from the normal work of acquisitions, but it is not, because only a well-informed service can know what is available and provide what is really needed. The skills needed for acquisitions have not really changed over time, but there is now a greater concentration on technology and a need to embrace change. The best acquisitions services will think first of their users and their institution, while trying to get the most out of the budget they have been given. They will exercise professional and unbiased judgement when it comes to choosing suppliers, and will keep communication open with them, being clear about what service they expect. They will continue to develop their service by being aware of developments and making the most of new opportunities offered, remaining as efficient as they can. Monitoring the service of suppliers, but also their own acquisitions operation, is part of continuing to be a viable and effective service. Acquisitions staff are still needed to locate and buy what our users need.

Further reading

Chapter 1

Introduction

Fisher, W. (2001) Core Competencies for the Acquisitions Librarian, *Library Collections, Acquisitions, and Technical Services*, **25**, 179–190.

Lugg, R. and Fischer, R. (2002) The Amazon Effect, Virtual Approval Plans, and the Changing Nature of Book Selection, *Against the Grain*, **14** (3), 1, 18, 20, 22.

Nagel, L. (2002) Biz of Acq – What Colour is Your Hat? Ethics in library–vendor relations, *Against the Grain*, **14** (1), 69–71.

Chapter 2

Pre-order checking

Brown, L. A. (1999) The Acquisitions Workstation – collection development style, *Against the Grain*, **11** (2), 1, 3, 16.

Gold, H. (2000) Acquisitions, the Internet and the Academic Library. In Timmons, M. E. (ed.), *The Internet and Acquisitions: sources and resources for development*, New York, Haworth.

Lee, S. and Shewring, P. (2001) Ordering New Books Fast and Furiously the Email Way, *Sconul Newsletter*, **23** (Summer/Autumn), 18–19.

Nicholas, D. et al. (2000) Got to Pick a Docket or Two: what is going on in the backwater that is bibliographic records?, *Library Association Record*, **102** (9), 508–9.

Wiegand, S. (2002) Incorporating Electronic Products into the Acquisitions Workflow in a Small College Library, *Library Collections, Acquisitions and Technical Services*, **26**, 363–6.

Chapter 3
Publishers and publishing

Bazirjian, R. and Nirnberger, B. (2003) Tracking Not Yet Published Material: using the bibliographic record the smart way, *Against the Grain*, **15** (1), 42, 44, 46–7.

Clark, G. (2001) *Inside Book Publishing*, 3rd edn, London, Routledge.

Healey, M. (2003) Think of a Number . . . we are running out of ISBNs, *Update*, **2** (6), 42–3.

Hunter, K. (2000) Publishing in 2000. In Chapman, E. and Lynden, F. (eds), *Advances in Librarianship*, **24**.

Chapter 4
Beyond the basic book

A change of form

Gelfand, J. (2000) Grey Literature Poses New Challenges for Research Libraries, *Collection Management*, **24** (1/2), 137–47.

Needham, P. (2002) MAGIC – shining a new light on a grey area, *Serials*, **15** (3), 201–6.

Pinfield, S. (2002) Creating Institutional E-print Repositories, *Serials*, **15** (3), 261–4.

Other collections

Dale, P. (ed.) (2004) *A Guide to Libraries and Information Sources in Government Departments and Other Organisations*, 34th edn, London, British Library, Science Reference and Information Service.

British government publications

Dawson, H. (2003) *Using the Internet for Political Research: practical tips and hints*, Oxford, Chandos.

Directory of EU Information Sources (2003) 13th edn, Brussels, Euroconfidentiel.

Refer. Journal of CILIP's Information Services Group has regular articles and knowledgeable updates on UK official publishing. It includes news from SCOOP, the Standing Committee on Official Publications, and is published three times per year.

Music

Duckles, V. H. and Reed, I. (eds) (1997) *Musical Reference and Research Materials: an annotated bibliography*, 5th edn, New York, Schirmer Books.

European music directory 2001 (2001) Saur.

Mixter, K. E. (1996) *General Bibliography for Music Research*, 3rd edn, Warren, MI, Harmonie Park Press.

New Grove Dictionary of Music and Musicians (2001) 2nd edn, London, Macmillan.

Penney, B. (1992) *Music in British Libraries: a directory of resources*, 4th edn, London, Library Association Publishing.

Audiovisual materials

Cooke, A. (2001) *A Guide to Finding Quality Information on the Internet*, 2nd edn, London, Library Association Publishing.

Gregory, V. L. (2000) *Selecting and Managing Electronic Resources: a how-to-do-it manual for librarians*, New York, Neal-Schuman.

Handman, G. (2003) Searching for the Seldom Seen: sources and strategies for acquiring out-of-distribution videos, *Against the Grain*, **15** (3), 42–4, 46.

Mason-Robinson, S. (1996) *Developing and Managing Video Collections: a how-to-do-it manual for librarians*, New York, Neal-Schuman.

Multimedia Information & Technology. Quarterly, published jointly by the Multimedia Group of Aslib and the Multimedia Information and Technology Group of CILIP.

Video librarian, www.videolibrarian.com.

Internet service additional to the journal *Video Librarian*, indexed reviews, news, distributors.

Chapter 5

Suppliers

Alessi, D. L. (2000) Raising the Bar: book vendors and the new realities of service, *Journal of Library Administration*, **28** (2), 25–40.

Ball, D. and Pye, J. (2000) Library Purchasing Consortia: their activity and effect on the marketplace. In Gorman, G., *Collection Management: International Yearbook of Library and Information Management 2000–2001*, London, Library Association Publishing.

Bills, L. (2000) Technical Services and Integrated Library Systems, *Library Hi Tech*, **18** (2), 144–50.

Coats, J. and Kiegel, J. (2003) Automating the Nexus of Book Selection, Acquisitions and Rapid Copy Cataloguing, *Library Collections, Acquisitions and Technical Services*, **27**, 33–44.

Flowers, J. and Perry, S. (2002) Vendor Assisted E-selection and Online Ordering: optimal conditions, *Library Collections, Acquisitions and Technical Services*, **26**, 395–407.

Kruse, T. and Holtzman, A. (2003) Web Booksellers – their usefulness to libraries, *Library Collections, Acquisitions and Technical Services*, **27** (1), 121–8.

Zhang, S., Miller, D. and Williams, J. (2002) Allocating the Technology Dividend in Technical Services through Using Vendor Services, *Library Collections, Acquisitions and Technical Services*, **26**, 379–93.

Chapter 6

Ordering

Congleton, R. (2002) Re-evaluating Technical Services Workflow for Integrated Library Systems, *Library Collections, Acquisitions and Technical Services*, **26**, 337–41.

Courtney, D. (2002) The Cloth–Paper Conundrum: the economics of simultaneous publication, *Journal of Scholarly Publishing*, **33** (4), 202–29.

Cromwell, D. (2002) ONIX and Electronic Ordering, *Technical Services Quarterly*, **20** (2), 54–7.

Rowsell, G. (2002) Automating Technical Services: an innovative approach in Australia, *Library Hi Tech*, **19** (3), 22–3.

Chapter 7

Out-of-the-ordinary ordering

Allen, C. G. (1999) *A Manual of European Languages for Librarians*, 2nd edn, New Providence, NJ, Bowker-Saur.

Bickers, P. (2002) New Ways to Acquire Old Books, *College and Research Libraries News*, **63** (3), 173–5.

Brantz, M. and Gray, D. (2003) Out of the Box and into the Bookstore: non-traditional use of the bookstore, *Against the Grain*, **15** (3), 36, 38, 40, 42.

Breaux, A.-M. (2001) Purchasing Continuations from a Monograph Vendor: some considerations, *Library Collections, Acquisitions and Technical Services*, **25**, 329–35.

Dillon, D. (2001) E-books: the University of Texas Experience, Part 1, *Library Hi Tech*, **19** (2), 113–24.

e-book Directory. Website providing free access e-books and links to sellers, www.ebookdirectory.com.

Flinchbaugh, M. (2001) Out-of-print Books: a practical, web-based solution, *Against the Grain*, **13** (1), 20, 22.

Galbraith, B. (2001) Evaluating Blackwell's Collection Manager as a Replacement for Approval Books, *Science and Technology Libraries*, **20** (4), 5–12.

Hurst, M. and Langendorfer, J. (2003) Comparison Shopping: purchasing continuations as standing orders or on approval, *Library Collections, Acquisitions and Technical Services*, **27** (2), 169–72.

Jaffe, N. (2002) The Library Marketplace – Print on Demand (POD): an important step in the change to a digital distribution model for books, *Against the Grain*, **14** (3), 72, 74–5.

Kellerman, L. (2002) Out of Print Digital Scanning: an acquisitions and preservation alternative, *Library Resources and Technical Services*, **46** (1), 3–10.

Langston, M. (2003) The California State University E-book Pilot Project: implications for cooperative collection development, *Library Collections, Acquisitions and Technical Services*, **27**, 19–32.

Lee, S. and Boyle, F. (2004) *Building an Electronic Resource Collection: a practical guide*, 2nd edn, London, Facet Publishing.

Machovec, G. (2003) netLibrary revisited review, *The Charleston Advisor*, **4** (4), 21–6.

Open book, useful website on e-books and standards, www.openbook.org/doc_library.htm.

Tafuri, N. (2003) A Good Book is Not That Hard to Find: librarians and the new out-of-print marketplace, *Against the Grain*, **15** (3), 18, 20, 22.

Vincelli, N. (2002) Online Auction Orders: an order librarian's reflections on OLAS, *Against the Grain*, **14** (4), 30, 32, 34.

Weatherford, R. (2003) Libraries and the Online Book World: where we have been and where we are going, *Against the Grain*, **15** (3), 27–8, 30, 32.

Chapter 8

When the orders arrive

Konshak, P. (2001) Coding a Custom Email Alert Service for New Books, *Computers in Libraries*, **21** (2), 24–6.

Chapter 9

Finance and budgets

Clayton, P. and Gorman, G. (2001) Budget Management. In *Managing Information Resources in Libraries and Information Services: collection management in theory and practice*, Chapter 8, London, Library Association Publishing.

Clayton, P. (2001) Managing the Acquisitions Budget: a practical perspective, *Bottom Line*, **14** (3), 145–51.

Kuo, H. (2001) Comparing Vendor Discounts for Firm Orders: fixed vs. sliding, *Technical Services Quarterly*, **18** (4), 1–10.

Lamborn, J. and Smith, P. (2001) Institutional Ties: developing an interface between a library acquisitions system and a parent institution accounting system, *Library Collections, Acquisitions and Technical Services*, **25**, 247–61.

Stevenson Smith, G. (2002) *Managerial Accounting for Libraries and Other Not-for-profit Organizations*, 2nd edn, Washington DC, ALA.

Chapter 10

The way ahead

The Acquisitions Librarian. Biannual, New York, Haworth, 1989–.

Against the Grain. Bimonthly, Charleston, S.C., Against the Grain, 1989–.

Anderson, R. (2001) Acquisitions in a Wired World: where are we going?, *Against the Grain*, **13** (1), 26, 28.

Chapman, L. (2000) Acquisitions: the emerging electronic paradigm. In *Collection Management: International Yearbook of Library and Information Management 2000–2001*, London, Library Association Publishing.

Clayton, P. and Gorman, G. (2001) (eds) *Managing Information Resources in Libraries and Information Services: collection management in theory and practice*, London, Library Association Publishing.

Clendenning, L. (2001) Crossing the Great Divide Between Acquisitions and Collections: selectors order online, *Against the Grain*, **12** (6), 85–6, 88.

Eaglen, A. (2000) *Buying Books: a how-to-do-it manual for librarians*, 2nd edn, New York, Neal Schuman.

Green, T. (2002) Can the Monograph Help Solve the Library Serials Funding Crisis?, *Serials*, **15** (2), 135–9.

Hurst, M. and Maurer, R. (2003) Library–Vendor Collaboration for Re-engineering Workflow: the Kent State experience, *Library Collections, Acquisitions and Technical Services*, **27** (2), 155–64.

Kenney, B. (2003) The Future of Integrated Library Systems, *Library Journal*, **128** (11), 36–40.

Kistler, J. (2001) Joys, Horrors, and the Future of Library Acquisitions, *Against the Grain*, **13** (5), 44, 46–7, 50, 52.

Library Collections, Acquisitions and Technical Services. Quarterly, New York, Elsevier, 1977–.

OCLC Library and information center (2003) *Five Year Information Format trends*, www.oclc.org/info/trends.

Schmidt, K. A. (ed.) (1999) *Understanding the Business of Library Acquisitions*, 2nd edn, Washington DC, ALA.

Taking Stock: libraries and the book trade. Twice per year, Madeley, NAG.

Wilkinson, F. and Lewis, L. (2003) *The Complete Guide to Acquisitions Management*, Westport, CT, Libraries Unlimited.

References

AcqWeb, acqweb.library.vanderbilt.edu.

Advanced Book Exchange, www.abebooks.com.

Agencia Espánola del ISBN, www.mcu.es.

ARIADNA (Spanish National Library catalogue), www.bne.es/esp/cat-fra.htm.

Aslib Directory of Information Sources in the United Kingdom (2002) 12th edn, London, Europa, Taylor & Francis Group.

AV-Online, US National Information Center for Educational Media (NICEM). CD-ROM or online.

BBC, www.bbcworldwide.com.

BIBLIODATA (German National Library catalogue), www.ddb.de.

Bibliofind.com, www.bibliofind.com, combined with Amazon.com.

Bibliografía Nacional Española, quarterly CD-ROM, London, Chadwyck-Healey.

Bibliografia Nacional Portuguesa, http://bnp.bn.pt.

Bibliografia Nazionale Italiana su CD-ROM, quarterly CD-ROM, Rome, Editrice Bibliografica, www.alice.it/eb/catalogo/cdrom.htm.

Bibliographie du Québec, www.bnquebec.ca.

Bibliographie Nationale Française, http://bibliographienationale.bnf.fr.

Bibliomania, www.bibliomania.com.

Bibliografía Nacional Española, quarterly, CD-ROM, National Library of Spain, London, Chadwyck-Healey.

Biblioteca Nacional, www.bn.pt.

BLPC (British Library Public Catalogue), www.bl.uk.

BN-OPALE see OPALE.

BNB see British National Bibliography.

Book Industry Communication, www.bic.org.uk.

BookFind-Online, annual web-based subscription service, Twickenham, Nielsen BookData.

Bookfinder.com, www.bookfinder.com.

Books in English, bimonthly cumulating microfiche, London, British Library. Ceases publication in 2004.

Booksinprint.com, www.booksinprint.com.

The Bookseller, weekly, Whitaker, 1933– , partial contents online, www.thebookseller.co.uk.

Booksellers' Association, *Bookshop Members Directory*. www.booksellers.org.uk/search. Also includes a useful directory of publishers.

Books Out of Print, www.booksoutofprint.com.

BookWise – CD-ROM, monthly subscription, Twickenham, Nielsen BookData.

Bookworld, www.bookworld.com.

Boosey, www.boosey.com.

BOPCAS (British Official Publications Current Awareness Service), www.bopcas.soton.ac.uk.

BOPCRIS (British Official Publications Collaborative Reader Information Service), www.bopcris.ac.uk.

Brazilian National Library Catalogue, www.bn.br.

British Catalogue of Music (*BCM*), semi-annual, New Providence, NJ, Bowker, 1957–.

British Library catalogues, www.bl.uk.

British National Bibliography (*BNB*), weekly with quarterly and annual cumulations (also available monthly on CD-ROM), London, British Library.

British Universities Film and Video Council, www.bufvc.ac.uk.

BUBL Information Service, www.bubl.ac.uk.

Catalogo dei Libri in Commercio (*ALICE*), monthly CD-ROM, New Providence, NJ, Bowker. An out-of-print service is also available.

Civil Service Yearbook (*CSYB*) (2003) 39th edn, TSO, www.civil-service.co.uk.

COBOP (Catalogue of British official publications not published by The Stationery Office), bimonthly with annual cumulations, TSO, 1980–.

Combined Higher Education Software Team (*CHEST*), www.chest.ac.uk.

Commonwealth Universities Yearbook, annual, London, Association of
    Commonwealth Universities, 1958–, www.acu.ac.uk.
Counterpoise, www.libr.org/AIP/bibtools.html.
Cybrary, University of Queensland website providing web access to national
    library catalogues, www.library.uq.edu.au/ssah/jeast.
Deutsche Nationalbibliographie Aktuell, CD-ROM, German National Library,
    1993–, www.ddb.de.
Directory of American Scholars (2001) 10th edn, Farmington Hills, MI, Gale.
Directory of Publishers [the red book] (2004) Twickenham, Nielsen BookData.
Directory of Special Libraries and Information Centers, annual, Farmington
    Hills, MI, Gale, 1963–.
*Directory of UK and Irish Publishers including Distributors, Sales Agents and
    Wholesalers*, London, Booksellers Association, www.booksellers.org.uk.
    Also available via BookWise as CD-ROM.
Directory of University Libraries in Europe (2004) 2nd edn, London, Europa,
    Taylor & Francis Group.
Europa, www.europa.eu.int/.
European Information Association, www.eia.org.uk.
Eurostat, www.europa.eu.int/comm/eurostat.
FACETS Catalog, www.facets.org.
French National Library catalogue see Gallica, OPALE.
Gabriel (gateway to Europe's national library websites), www.bl.uk/gabriel/.
Gallica (French National Library catalogue of digitized texts),
    www.gallica.bnf.fr.
German National Library catalogue see BIBLIODATA.
Global Books in Print, Bowker, 1990–, www.globalbooksinprint.com.
GODORT, www. sunsite.berkeley.edu/GODORT/.
Guide to Microforms in Print (2003) Farmington Hills, MI, Gale.
Guide to Reprints (2003) Farmington Hills, MI, Gale.
Gutenberg Project, www.gutenberg.net.
half.com, www.half.ebay.com.
HERON (Higher Education Resources On Demand), www.heron.ingenta.com/.
HMSO, www.hmso.gov.uk.
ICOLC (International Coalition of Library Consortia),
    www.library.yale.edu/consortia.

Inside, www.bl.uk/services/current/inside.html.

International Guide to Microform Masters (1997) Farmington Hills, MI, Gale.

International Literary Market Place see Literary Market Place.

International Who's Who of Authors and Writers, annual, London, Europa, Taylor & Francis Group.

Internet Movie Database (information on 100,000+ movies, including a categorized list of newsgroups and listservs), www.uk.imdb.com.

Italian Books in Print (2002), Munich, Saur.

Italian National Library catalogue see SBN Italian National Library catalogue.

Karlsruher Virtueller Katalog, www.ubka.uni-karlsruhe.de/kvk.html.

KnowEurope, www.knoweurope.net.

Libraries and Information Services in the United Kingdom and the Republic of Ireland, annual, London, Facet Publishing.

Library of Congress, *Music Catalog*, quarterly, CD-ROM, online, Washington DC, Library of Congress.

Libros Españoles en Venta ISBN, irregular, Instituto Nacional, available at del libro Español, 1984–, www.mcu.es/bases/spa/isbn/ISBN.html.

LibWeb, web-based annual subscription service, Twickenham, Nielsen BookData.

Lightning Source Inc, www.lightningsource.com.

LISUa, *Annual Library Statistics Featuring Trend Analysis of UK Public and Academic Libraries*, annual, Loughborough, LISU.

LISUb, *Average Prices of British and USA Academic Books*, biannual, Loughborough, LISU.

Literary Market Place (includes International Literary Market Place), annual, CD-ROM, New Providence, NJ, Bowker Electronic Publishing, www.infotoday.com.

Livres Disponibles (French books in print), annual, Paris, Electra, 1977–, www.electra.com.

Livres Hebdo, weekly, Paris, Editions professionnelles du livre, 1979–, www.electre.com.

Media Review Digest, www.pieranpress.com/index.php/.

MP3, www.mp3.com.

Music Publishers' International ISMN Directory (2004) 5th edn, Munich, Saur.

National Acquisitions Group (2003) *Directory of Acquisitions Librarians in the*

United Kingdom and Republic of Ireland, 8th edn, Maberley, NAG.

National Faculty Directory (2003) 34th edn, Farmington Hills, MI, Gale.

National Union Catalog, Washington DC, Library of Congress. Library of Congress current catalogue, www.loc.gov/.

NetLibrary, www.netlibrary.com.

OECD (Organisation for Economic Cooperation and Development), www.oecd.org.

OPALE (French National Library catalogue), www.bnf.fr/.

Open Government, www.open.gov.uk.

Österreichische Bibliographie (Austrian national bibliography), http://bibliographie.onb.ac.at/biblio/.

Parliament, www.parliament.uk.

PORBASE, www.porbase.org.

Portuguese National Library catalogue *see Biblioteca Nacional*.

Premier-CD, double disk monthly subscription, Twickenham, Nielsen BookData.

Publishers' Directory (2003) 26th edn, Farmington Hills, MI, Gale.

Publishers, Distributors and Wholesalers of the US (2000) 22nd edn, New Providence, NJ, Bowker.

Publishers' International ISBN Directory (2003/4) 30th edn, Munich, Saur.

Publishers' International ISBN Directory Plus (2003) 8th edn, CD-ROM, Farmington Hills, MI, Gale.

Publishers Weekly, Bowker, 1872–. Partial contents, www.publishersweekly.reviewsnews.com/.

RED (Retail Entertainment Data Publishing), www.redpublishing.co.uk/.

Reel.com (information on movie DVDs searchable by title, actor, director or genre), www.reel.com.

RISM (Répertoire International des Sources Musicales), 7th edn, CD-ROM, New Providence, NJ, Bowker-Saur.

RLG (Research Libraries Group) *Union Catalog*, www.rlg.org/libres.html.

SBN Italian National Library catalogue, www.bncf.firenze.sbn.it/.

Scholarly Societies Project, www.scholarly-societies.org/.

Sessional Information Digest, annual, TSO (publication often delayed: 1998/99 volume published in 2000).

SIGLE (System for Information on Grey Literature in Europe), www.stn-international.de/stndatabases/databases/sigle.html.

Spanish Books in Print online, New Providence, NJ, Bowker, www.spanishbooksinprint.com.

Spanish National Library catalogue *see ARIADNA*.

The Red Book: directory of publishers (2004) Twickenham, Nielsen BookData.

The Stationery Office catalogue, Norwich, TSO, www.tso.co.uk.

UKOP *Online* (United Kingdom Official Publications), web or CD-ROM subscription, daily online updates, Norwich, The Stationery Office, www.ukop.co.uk.

UN United Nations, www.un.org.

US Government Printing Office (USGPO), www.gpoaccess.gov.

Verzeichnis Lieferbarer Bücher (VLB), annual, print or CD-ROM, Munich, Saur, www.buchhandel.de.

Video Sourcebook (2003) 31st edn, Farmington Hills, MI, Gale.

Viewfinder, www.bufvc.ac.uk/publications/viewfinder.html.

Whitaker's directory of publishers see The Red Book.

Who's Who, annual, print or CD-ROM, London, A & C Black Ltd.

World Guide to Libraries (2004) 18th edn, print or CD-ROM, Farmington Hills, MI, Gale.

World Guide to Special Libraries (2003) 6th edn, Farmington Hills, MI, Gale.

The World of Learning, annual, print or online, London, Europa Publications, Taylor & Francis Group.

WorldCat (subscription service from OCLC FirstSearch), www.oclc.org.

The Writers' Directory, annual, London, St James Press.

Zetoc, British Library service available to ac.uk addresses and English NHS organizations and NHS Scotland, http://zetoc.mimas.ac.uk.

Glossary

AACR2	Anglo-American Cataloguing Rules, 2nd edition
accession number	running number assigned to acquisitions on arrival
AcqWeb	internet resource for acquisitions
aggregator	intermediary supplier that brings together diverse electronic materials for sale
ALA	American Library Association
approval plan	materials sent according to an agreed profile – those not required can be returned
ARL	Association of Research Libraries (USA)
backlist	older titles still in print in publisher's list
BFI	British Film Institute
bibliographic data	information defining a specific title
BIC	Book Industry Communication (UK)
BL	British Library
blanket order	order for all publications in an agreed area or from one publisher with no returns anticipated
blurb	publisher's enthusiastic description of material
BNB	British National Bibliography
bookbot	e-commerce robot which searches for books on the internet
bookmark	method of marking your place in a book or on the internet
browser	computer program, including tools, which can search the WWW
BUBL	electronic bulletin board for libraries

BUFVC	British Universities Film and Video Council
bundling	selling several (electronic) products together as a group
CD-ROM	compact disc – read-only memory
CHEST	UK Combined Higher Education Software Team, part of EDUSERVE the UK educational charity
CILIP	Chartered Institute of Library and Information Professionals (UK)
CIP	Cataloguing in Publication, provided pre-publication
claim	request to send outstanding orders
consortium	agreed grouping of services to organize advantageous purchasing deals
continuation	subsequent volumes or parts in an ongoing numbered series
copyright	legal right to publish an item
copyright library	library which receives one copy of all items published in that country
COPAC	CURL Online Public Access Catalogue
credit	money paid to acquisitions because of wrong delivery, non-delivery or discount
CURL	Consortium of University Research Libraries in the UK
CWO	cash with order
data streaming	continuous transfer of data to support high level computer applications
deposit account	account in which acquisitions department lodges money in anticipation of purchases
desiderata	list of wanted items, often but not always out of print
Dewey	classification for arrangement of items in a collection

discount	reduction in price, usually a percentage, sometimes negotiable
domain name	*see* URL
download	transfer electronic data between computers
DVD	digital versatile (or video) disc for storing movies/sound
EAN	European Article Numbering system
e-book	electronic text read either on a special hand-held device, a hand-held computer or other computer
e-commerce	trade using the internet
EDI	Electronic Data Interchange – standardized computer communication
EDIteur	EDI group for the USA and other countries
EDIFACT	UN rules for EDI
electronic invoice	paperless invoicing
electronic ordering	paperless ordering
EU	European Union
format	physical appearance of material, e.g. book, microform, DVD
fund accounting	division of a budget into discrete areas
gathering	group of pages brought together for binding
HERON	Higher Education Resources on Demand Project, part of Ingenta
HMSO	Her Majesty's Stationery Office
ICOLC	International Coalition of Library Consortia
ICT	information and communications technology
ILS	Integrated Library System
imprint	statement of publishing details or name of publisher
in print	material currently available from publisher
internet	interlinked computer networks which allow access to each other
IP address	Internet Protocol address
ISBN	International Standard Book Number
ISMN	International Standard Music Number

ISO	International Standards Organization
ISRC	International Standard Recording Code
ISSN	International Standard Serial Number
JSTOR	Journal STORage system in USA, accessed internationally
LC	Library of Congress (USA)
LCSH	Library of Congress Subject Headings
library supplier	specialist supplier variously known as a bookseller, vendor, jobber, agent
licence	written contract, often relating to digital materials, governing conditions of use
LISU	Library and Information Statistics Unit at Loughborough University
MARC	Machine Readable Cataloguing
megasearch engine	large search engine
metadata	data about data
microform	reduced photographic document copy which requires a special reader but little storage space or conservation
monograph	single published item, usually a book
MP3	compressed digital sound for speedy downloading from the internet
NAG	National Acquisitions Group (UK)
Nesli	National Electronic Site Licensing Initiative (UK)
Net	the internet
NISC	National Information Services Corporation
NUC	National Union Catalog (USA)
NYP	not yet published
OCLC	Online Center for Library Cooperation (USA)
OD	out of distribution
OECD	Organisation for Economic Cooperation and Development
OP	out of print
OPAC	Online Public Access Catalogue

open archives	electronic databases usually allowing unrestricted access and use
outsourcing	using an outside organization to do in-house work
PA	Publishers Association (UK)
periodical	*see* serial
prepayment	payment at the time of ordering
print on demand	immediate reprinting of an out-of-print book
print-run	number of copies of a title printed at one time
pro forma	invoice to be paid before delivery of order
quango	semi-public administrative body appointed by government outside the civil service
remainders	unsold copies of material available at discount
reprint	reprinting of material in new or same form
returns	items returned to publisher (or supplied) for refund
RLG	Research Libraries Group
RLIN	Research Libraries Information Network
SAN	Standard Address Number for e-commerce partners
SCONUL	Society of National and University Libraries (UK)
search engine	online software to search internet databases
serial	publication appearing regularly in separate parts
service charge	extra payment for material with minimal discount
shelf-ready	items processed/labelled by supplier ready to put straight into stock
simultaneous publication	publication of the same material in two countries at the same time, e.g. UK and USA
SISAC	serial item identifier presented in barcode form
standing order	pre-order for all successive items in a series such as annuals
STM	scientific, technical, medical publishing
streaming	*see* data streaming

subscription (sub)	pre-payment for all parts of a serial, usually paid annually
teleordering	method of e-commerce transfer of information
TSO	The Stationery Office – UK government publisher
UN	United Nations
URL	Uniform Resource Locator – internet site address, also known as domain name
voucher	request for payment in accounting systems
website	address or location on the internet
WWW	world wide web, the web

Index